Yogurt & Sou

THE

SIMPLER LIFE

COOKBOOK

FROM

ARROWHEAD MILLS

BY FRANK FORD

The Simpler Life Cookbook

Copyright 1974
by Harvest Press, Inc.
Post Office Box 3535
Fort Worth, Texas 76105

Printed in the United States of America
First Printing - October 1974 - 23,000
Second Printing - February 1976 - 17,000
Third Printing - September 1976 - 110,000

This book is the third edition of a book which was originally released under the title of *Pack to Nature*.

DEDICATION

This book is dedicated to my wife Margie, who not only cooks natural foods well with a loving and cheerful spirit, but also transformed the enclosed recipes into a readable wholeness. Thanks, also, to Dave, who did the tractor work while this was being written; Cindy, who typed and organized; and Dan and Susan, who kept the household going during the entire project.

INTRODUCTION

I met Frank in 1968, detouring to Hereford while traveling cross-country wanting to meet the man who was supplying organically grown grains and beans for my natural foods store in San Francisco. Warm, honest, intelligent, humorous — it sure was easy to make friends with Frank. His business was already ten years old then — gritty, elemental like the surrounding prairie, just Frank and his helper, Ken Duncan, and just beginning to break even financially. But I hadn't expected anything big or fancy; I was pleased because my supplier had integrity. Frank was an organic farmer because he believed it was better for his land and for you and me to farm that way and, since he appreciated the uniqueness of his work, he wanted to preserve the integrity of his crops by marketing them himself. He had a simple vision: quality always wins a following, therefore Arrowhead would be a winner.

How marvelously his vision has been vindicated, his patience and diligence rewarded! Arrowhead Mills still operates the original stone mill, the battered old truck still backs up to the little loading dock of the weathered, original old building. But now there are also 8 new mills, 5 trucks and trailers, 150,000 square feet of manufacturing, processing, packaging, warehouse and office space.

Ken Duncan, now one of 47 employees, has grown to executive status — Vice President, Production — and into ownership of the company, one of 22 shareholders. There are more than 30 Arrowhead organic growers farming more than 60,000 acres, 44 natural foods distributors bring more than 350 Arrowhead products to thousands of stores throughout every state of the U.S.

Even more exciting than Arrowhead's tremendous victory for Frank's business life is the victory that God has won for his spiritual life. Frank made Jesus Christ lord of his life 3 years ago and that's when love and joy began to transform his life by the living power of God's Holy Spirit. God is carrying on a great work in his life, transforming an organic farmer into an organic man, integrating him body, soul and spirit, transforming Arrowhead Mills from a work of man into a work of God. The same miracle of God's grace has transformed my life, enabling me to understand what Frank means when he says, "Arrowhead Mills belongs to God." When Jesus Christ becomes lord of your life, He becomes Lord of your *whole* life — the word "organic" is elevated to its rightful level of descriptive power. In 1968 it was impossible to talk about Frank Ford without talking

about Arrowhead Mills; in 1975 it's impossible to talk about him without talking about
God. But he's still living right here on planet
Earth, generously sharing his knowledge of
the good things of our earth, comfortable as
farmer, businessman, evangelist or the writer
who teaches us how to lead a simpler life.

Fred Rohé
Shiloh Farms
Sulphur Springs, Ark.
December, 1975

PROLOGUE

Over the years, it has never ceased to amaze me how simple and inexpensive it is to feed a hungry group in the canoe country of Canada or in the mountains of New Mexico. Whole natural food staples and fresh garden vegetables taste good anywhere, but I must admit that they taste even better under those conditions.

It seems to me that there are probably a lot of people who would like to eat better, spend less time and money in doing so, and keep life as simple and uncomplicated as possible. The recipes included in this book use whole food staples that are nutritious, easy to store without refrigeration, easy to prepare, and, hopefully, good tasting to you and your family.

These are the standards, too, which we have held through the years here at Arrowhead Mills. After seven years with an old pick-up and trailer delivering the stoneground flour and cornmeal produced with one 30 inch stonegrinder, the little company finally broke even. A year or so later, the young people of this country began to infuse talent and enthusiasm into what later became known as the natural foods movement.

A foundation was being laid for the times we now see coming. A viable network of people who know how to live close to the soil, to sleep in the back of a truck, on the floor of a warehouse, or in the woods, began to develop nutritionally-sound products and exchange information about grains, beans, seeds and other whole foods being grown by farmers who are trying to improve their soil and work in harmony with nature's laws.

With the costs of synthesized fertilizers skyrocketing, the farmer who has been using composted manure and other natural materials in his soil is looking a little smarter. He has billions of soil bacteria and earthworms out in the fields developing the fertility and tilth he needs to produce good crops.

While total reliance on pesticides has been building up immunity in the insects which threaten crops and at the same time destroying the predator insects such as the ladybug, trichogramma, and lacewing fly which can keep things under control, some farmers have been using these beneficial insects with the result of less expense and cleaner food.

While many commercial food processors have literally been stripping away all the health-giving qualities of the foods they handle, and then putting huge advertising budgets behind the over packaged non-food that results, others have been quietly learning more about ways in which we can return to the whole foods which were once our heritage.

There is a rapidly increasing interest in home gardening and in maintaining a rotated reserve supply of these home-processed foods as well as purchased grains and other storable foods. Even the city dweller, high above busy streets, can plant a little herb garden in pots along the window sill and sprout mungbeans and alfalfa seed. A reserve supply of food and water is especially important in the cities.

Exciting times lie ahead of us. They have been prophesied for two thousand years and more. The Word says we are to occupy until He comes. I hope that this little book will help you to do that.

Frank Ford

Table
of
CONTENTS

CLOTHING AND EQUIPMENT FOR THE WOODS

. If a person is just on an overnight camping trip, about the worst thing that can happen from being ill prepared in most places is hunger and discomfort. If a person is going to be out close to nature for an extended period of time, much prior planning is necessary. Depending on the locale, shelter and clothing needs will vary, but this check list would be basic in any event, with supplies of each dependent upon the time you plan to stay:

- adequate outdoor clothing: hiking boots, rainwear, winter clothing, plenty of socks and underwear.

- a good bedroll (better to have one summer, one winter).

- air mattress or foam pad.

- poncho (suitable for ground cloth, rainwear, or shelter).

- cooking equipment (light grill, skillets, pots, plates, cups, forks, knives, spoons, cleaning pads, can opener, special utensils, large pots or tub for washing, etc.)

- lightweight towels and washrags (easier to wash and dry).

- plenty of soap (for personal hygiene, washing dishes and clothes).

- personal toilet articles, toothpaste, etc.

- matches (large supply, packed in waterproof containers).

- toilet paper and paper towels (must also be kept dry).

- first aid kit.

- condiments (all seasonings and herbs which you wish to use).

- bucksaw (large enough and in sharp condition).

- axe (both large and small — need training in use of).

- hoe, shovel, rake (many uses around a campsite).

- file and whetstone for sharpening equipment.

- good knives of various sizes (kept sharp).

- lightweight fishing equipment if one plans to fish (poles can be cut, but you need plenty of light line and hooks).

- lantern, spare fuel and mantles - candles.

- flashlights, reserve supply of batteries.

- plenty of rope, both heavy and lightweight.

- plenty of twine and wire.

- good tentage, preferable in most cases to have a large floored tent of heavy construction for extended camp.

- small mountain tent, lightweight for backpacking (see backpacking).

- backpack (you will want to make some forays out from base camp — there are many good styles available).

- a good chuckbox for storing condiments, matches, papers, etc.

➤ - tool kit.

➤ - a good book on edible wild plants (see recommended books).

➤ - several other things which you have probably thought of.

➤ - storable food supply (grains, beans, seeds, sprouting jars, dried fruits, freeze dried vegetables, herb teas, hand grinder).

> In considering food for storage, it will pay you to stay with the basics. God made grains, beans and seeds for your use (Gen. 1:29). They can be stored indefinitely, kept cool and dry, with a light application of diatomaceous earth* dusted into the grain to keep out insect activity. Grains, beans and seeds have the advantage of being live food. The most advantageous way to use them is sprouting (see sprouting chart). This increases vitamin content and enzyme activity which is very beneficial to health.

Backpacking.— It is hard to find better companionship or environmental concern than among those hardy folks who like to backpack in the high country. Lightweight, specialized equipment is necessary, and any member of your local Sierra Club can put you in touch with the right sources. It is my purpose here to discuss briefly the food available for backpacking. Freeze-dried and other trail foods are available in cans at a fraction of the cost which has often been paid for environment-polluting small throw-away packaging. We here at Arrowhead Mills have been putting together those foods which are the most quality for the least cost, and which are produced by people who have a concern for total environment.

---

*Diatomaceous earth is merely a finely powdered tiny sea shell material which is not harmful at all to the human digestive system. Just leave it in grain as it is just a good source of minerals.

Those foods which lend themselves well to backpacking include our delicious Maple-Nut Granola, dried fruits, nuts, corn munchies, grain flakes, and various freeze-dried foods. It is a very simple matter to transfer just the right amount of these foods from your cupboard into small, reusable bags and cut your food costs in half while supporting environmental awareness. By getting your friends to do the same, you can use up the larger supplies rather quickly.

But whether you are a backpacker, a car camper, a person who would like to pack to nature for an extended time, or perhaps just enjoy good whole foods in your home, I hope that you will study the basic foods list and that the recipe ideas in this book will be of help.

For information on *The Simpler Life* reserve foods storage program, write to: Arrowhead Mills, Box 866, Hereford, Texas 79045.

YOU AND THE TOTAL ENVIRONMENT

Over the past few years, there has been an increasing awareness on the part of many people about the need to conserve our natural resources and protect the quality of life on this planet. We are slowly realizing the need to reduce our demands upon the ecosystem and live in closer harmony with God's laws.

There are many ways that we can contribute to this awareness. Some involve social action and community effort. Many involve only the way we live as individuals. Here are a few brief thoughts for you to consider if you would like to help conserve some nature to "pack to".

With regard to camping, I highly recommend that you travel as light as possible consistent with the length of your stay. One can move quietly into a camping area, put up a tent and enjoy the fragrance of the forest without the weight, worry and hassle of a lot of heavy and expensive equipment.

Fire pits should be kept away from trees or other ignitable material, and should be closed after the fire is carefully extinguished when leaving. Firewood should be fallen timber or dead limbs sawed carefully from the trees. Growing trees or bushes should never be cut. All trash should be gathered from the area before you leave — even that which you did not drop. Where trash cans are not provided, the trash should be carried out with you..

If you are going to be near water, you might consider the joy of sailing, rowing and canoeing. Even on larger lakes, there are usually quiet arms of the lake on which to enjoy such. Life preservers should always be worn, and the simple, coastguard approved models are very inexpensive. They will double as a nice pillow at night.

In the cities where most folks live, we can help our environment by using public conveyances when possible, and by riding a bicycle or walking more. Most of us do not get enough exercise anyway. In these times of energy shortages (and we should not be lulled into a false sense of security about energy availability), we should use car pools and reduce driving as much as possible.

And speaking of energy, does it really make sense to ignore the use of our natural fertilizer materials in crop production, then take the food and spend valuable energy stripping away most of the nutrition in the processing of highly refined foods? It takes energy to put the de-natured remainder into high-cost packaging. It takes energy to move it to market. It takes energy for the shopper to go get it at the store. And then — much of it produces no energy at all when eaten.

As a matter of fact, if soaring medical expenses and increasing sickness in our supposedly enlightened and modern society are any indicators, the terrible waste involved in highly processed and refined foods does not end at the super-market shelf. This waste becomes a tragedy in the lives of millions of American children, if their teeth and over-all health is a measure of their diet.

Many of our rivers and much of the life-giving forces in the oceans are already dead. We should consider how each of our daily acts contributes to the heavy load of pollution which our soil, water, air — and our bodies — must absorb. If we are to be stewards of our earth, we should utilize our natural resources effectively and correctly.

But most importantly, we as a nation have not used the spiritual resources which have been given so abundantly by our Creator.

Our bodies, which the Word calls the "Temple of the Holy Spirit", have been abused with the rest of our environment because we as individuals and as a nation have failed to repent, to accept His grace, and to live in the power of His Spirit. Earthly resources are running out, but the resources available to us from our Lord are limitless. He has made over 7,000 promises to us. One of these promises is 2nd Chronicles 7:14: "If my people ... will turn from their wicked ways ... I will heal their land."

Many families are becoming interested in organic gardening these days. By using companion plantings such as marigolds, onions or garlic to reduce the insect problem and by composting their soil, they are finding that they can enjoy quality produce from their own yard, and at the same time help to nourish the fragile web of life that covers our earth home.

Organic Gardening and Farming magazine (see recommended books, page 152) is an excellent source of practical experience and interesting ideas. For information on a unique kitchen waste composter, write Cinagro Distributors, P. O. Box 13821, Atlanta, Georgia, 30324 (see Source List, page 153).

Write Arrowhead Mills
    Box 866
    Hereford, Texas 79045
for free information on Gardens and Grains Preparation Program.

Basic Foods for Good Nutrition

Wheat, hard red winter — There is an age-old saying that "It takes nine months to make wheat or man". Because the hard red winter wheat grown in Deaf Smith County takes nine months from seed to crop, the roots have time to go deep into the mineral-rich subsoil of this area, producing a grain which has been noted for its protein, vitamin and mineral content. Wheat is the basic food of Western civilization.

Rye — This excellent grain is often used for variety in breads, and while it does not have the gluten content of wheat, and therefore does not rise like wheat bread, it does have an excellent taste. Rye is grown on the high plains of Eastern Colorado as well as in the Deaf Smith County area.

Yellow Corn — Many people now own their own hand grinders, and grind their own grits, meal or flour fresh each day. The corn, wheat or rye from the Deaf Smith County area usually runs much higher in protein than USDA standards. Yellow corn is high in Vitamin A, and makes a delicious meal. Corn and beans have been the staple foods of much of the Western Hemisphere.

White Corn — White corn does not have the Vitamin A content of yellow corn, but it has an excellent taste and is good for making hominy and corn tortillas. The corn grits which can be coarse ground from either white or yellow corn can be a delicious addition to almost any meal, and is easily prepared as mush or as part of any number of dishes.

Brown Rice, Long and Medium Grain — Most commercially available rice has not only been grown with practices potentially very damaging to the environment, but has also been polished with a process removing much of its B-Vitamin and mineral content.

The brown rice grown in Texas and Louisiana with sound agricultural practices is nutritious, and is a delight to prepare in soups, casseroles, and many other dishes.

Brown Rice, Short Grain — This famous rice is grown in California by a dedicated farm family. It is more glutenous than long and medium grain, and has a delicious flavor. Rice has long been the staple food of the Far East as well as a much-appreciated delicacy throughout the world. It is easily digestible as well as nutritious, and lends itself to many uses, including baby food.

Triticale — This is a true grain, not a hybrid, which has been developed from hard red winter wheat, durham wheat, and rye. It is slightly higher in protein than wheat, and has a better amino-acid balance than many grains. As it is low in gluten, it should be mixed with wheat flour for bread, but it makes an excellent pancake mix, cereal, whole or sprouted grain for good nutrition.

Wheat, soft — Soft wheat is used for pastry flour, and its smooth texture can be used in many dishes, from the batter for tempura vegetables, to the finest cakes and pie-crusts. It is a different grain than hard red winter wheat in that it has a softer, fatter kernel, and the specialized uses listed above.

Buckwheat Groats — Buckwheat is grown in the Pennsylvania — New York area. The best grains, after hulling, are sold as groats. White buckwheat groats are unroasted and brown groats are those which have been roasted. Buckwheat is high in B Vitamins, and is highly regarded for use in many dishes as well as flour for pancakes.

Millet, hulled — Known as the "Poor Man's Rice" in

much of the world, Millet is a very nutritious, low-gluten grain. It is grown in North Dakota and Colorado, and makes a good ingredient in soups and stews as well as a breakfast cereal. It is a staple food in Africa, China and Japan.

Barley, pearled — Barley has a tight-fitting hull which is removed by the process called "pearling". It is grown in the Red River Valley of North Dakota and Minnesota, and is pearled as lightly as possible to remove the fibrous hull, yet leave maximum nutrition. Barley is delicious in soups and casseroles.

Soybeans — Grown in China for 3,000 years, soybeans are now grown so extensively in the U. S. that three-quarters of the world production is now in this country. Deaf Smith County soybeans have been found to be higher than the usual 34% average protein, and are high in vitamins, minerals and unsaturated fats. Soybeans should be cooked or sprouted to destroy the urease and antitrypsin enzymes which interfere with digestion.

Mungbeans — These small beans are used almost exclusively for sprouting, have a high germination rate, and are very easy to sprout. Information on sprouting is listed in this book. The delicious, crisp sprouts can be used in cooked vegetable dishes (especially Chinese dishes), soup and salads.

Black-eyed Peas — Like other legumes, black-eyed peas are excellent soil builders. They take the nitrogen from the air and convert it into soil nitrogen through nodules on the roots. Black-eyed peas originated in Asia, and are a favorite dish of many people, both by themselves, and as an ingredient in soups or stews.

Lima Beans — First grown in tropical America, lima beans, like other beans and peas, are a good source of protein. Better utilization of protein is obtained by eating beans and grain dishes in the same meal. The essential amino acids are generally brought into better balance by combining grains and beans.

Lentils — The most famous lentil growing areas of the United States are Western Idaho and the neighboring area in Washington State. Lentils are an excellent source of protein, and have a variety of uses, including sprouting. As a cooked bean, they are often used in soups and casseroles.

Garbanzos (also known as Chickpeas) — This legume is a traditional food of the Middle East. Like most beans, they are a good course of protein, minerals and vitamins. They are raised in Mexico and in California and are often used in soups, patés, vegetable dishes and salads.

Sesame Seeds — Rich in Protein, unsaturated oils, and calcium, the Sesame seed is grown in Mexico and Central America. It makes a good complimentary addition to many beans and breads, and is the source of the high quality cooking oil favored by many cooks.

Sunflower Seeds, hulled — One of the nice things about sunflower seeds is that they are not only very high in protein, unsaturated oils and minerals, but also they are delicious as a snack or as an addition to an almost unlimited number of dishes. They can be included in breads, cookies, main dishes, salads and home-made granola.

Alfalfa Seeds — While a package of alfalfa seeds might seem expensive at first glance, people who have seen how much delicious sprout salad can come from a spoonful of seed are turning more and more to this easy-to-sprout seed for healthful salads. The seed, grown in North Texas near the Red River, have been thoroughly cleaned and checked for germination rate.

Peanuts — Just 80 miles southwest of Deaf Smith County, the famous Valencia peanuts are grown in an average of 350 days of sunshine a year. They are the sole ingredient in the Deaf Smith brand peanut butter which has set a new standard for taste and quality in the industry. Peanuts are a legume, and are rich in protein, unsaturated oil, and of course — taste.

Almonds — Grown in California by a dedicated group of growers, almonds have been called the "King of Nuts". They are nutritious as well as a tasty snack. All nuts are a good source of protein. Slivered almonds are often used in granola as well as many other recipes.

Pecan Halves — Native pecans have grown for years without the pesticide technology of man, and these native pecans, from Eastland County area of Texas have a solid, high protein, meat and a taste that makes them a welcome after-school snack as well as an ingredient in many delicious dishes.

Cracked Wheat Cereal — This cereal is a hearty meal that costs only a few cents. Prepared by cracking grains of hard red winter wheat into approximately 6 or 8 easy-to-cook particles, cracked wheat cereal is a favorite with children. Whole grain nutrition is a good way to start off the day.

Bulghur-Soy Grits — Bulghur-soy grits are a combination of two basic foods - bulghur, which is wheat which has been partially cooked under pressure, and the versatile soybean, which furnishes additional protein. The nutty flavor of these two together makes for a delicious breakfast or side dish.

Wheat Flakes — These flakes, made with the Deaf Smith hard red winter wheat, are produced with a unique flaking system which utilizes a short-duration dry-radiant heat which partially cooks the grains while at the same time preserving vitamins and minerals. They are easily stored, kept cool and dry, and quickly prepared in many ways. They are also a good snack just as they come from the package.

Rye Flakes — As rye is used less than wheat in breads and other baked goods, the use of these nutritious rye flakes in soups, main dishes and granola-type cereals is a good way to take advantage of the many fine qualities of rye. The dry-radiant flaking method has been tested and found to retain the nutrition of the whole grain.

Triticale Flakes — The outstanding nutrition available in this new grain, along with the taste of these dry-radiant produced flakes, makes this a favorite for inexpensive, yet delicious, eating. These flakes can be used in a vast variety of soups, casseroles, and other nutritious dishes which are easy to prepare.

Soybean Flakes — Arrowhead Soy Flakes are also prepared by the dry-radiant process. Those who have been discouraged by the long cooking times of whole soybeans have made these meaty flakes a favorite for many types of main dishes. The high protein of soybeans makes this a real food bargain at a fraction of the cost of other protein foods. Inventive and budget-conscious cooks have made these soy flakes a staple in their kitchens.

Maple Nut Granola — The careful roasting of a tasty blend of wheat, rye and oat flakes, sliced filberts and almonds, sunflower seeds and sesame seeds and just the right amount of corn germ oil, all in a generous portion of pure maple syrup from New England, with raisins added lavishly after baking, has made this ready-to-eat cereal a favorite for snackers, packers and all kinds of other folks. Good on ice cream or yogurt.

Stoneground Whole Wheat Flour — The careful stone grinding of the best quality wheat available has made the art of home baking with whole wheat flour come alive again. The delightful aroma of bread dough rising in the kitchen or baking in the oven gives the whole family an incentive to be close by when the bread comes out of the oven. Olde Mill Stone Ground Flour is a favorite in many homes.

Stoneground Rye Flour — An interesting and tasty change of pace can be accomplished in the oven with a Swedish or Italian Rye Bread. Rye flour can be mixed with whole wheat or with cornmeal to make some interesting pancakes, too. The unique flavor of rye has made this flour a respected member of the flour bin group.

Stoneground yellow cornmeal — It even makes fish taste much better, say the fishermen. But stoneground cornmeal is at its best when it is in a tasty cornbread steaming under some butter and perhaps topped off with honey.

Stoneground white cornmeal — Some folks like the subtle taste of white cornmeal. Easy to prepare cornbread, along with some steaming pinto beans has carried many a day for those who know good taste and good nutrition. Some say that buttermilk sure goes good with this combination.

Triticale Flour — Fast becoming a favorite with many people for a mix with wholewheat flour in breads or for use in pancakes and waffles, triticale flour provides the good nutrition of whole grains along with a unique taste provided by the wheat and rye from which it was developed.

Soy Flour — Olde Mill Soy Flour has been lightly roasted to improve its digestibility and flavor. The soybeans are roasted by dry-radiant heat and then ground into fine flour. Soy flour is a good protein ingredient for almost any bread or pancake, and can be used in many other dishes as well.

Raw Wheat Germ — Wheat germ is the embryo of the wheat kernel, and is responsible for carrying the spark of life to the next generation of wheat. Likewise, it is considered a very nutritious addition .to bread doughs, cereals, casseroles, salads, or main dishes.

Whole Wheat Pasta — Noodles, spaghetti, and other pasta made from special types of whole wheat flour and variations made with rice and soy flours make up a line of easily stored, nutritious food which can be easily prepared at a moment's notice. Many interesting dishes can be prepared with pasta as the base.

Tamari Soy Sauce — This soy sauce, made with soybeans, wheat and sea salt, naturally fermented, and aged in wood for two years, is a delicious addition to vegetables, casseroles, soups, grain dishes, or salads. It is a live food, made without artificial chemicals and preservatives common to commercial "soy sauce". Tamari soy sauce is used often in the following recipes because it adds nutrition as well as taste.

Sea Salt — Unrefined sea-salt, which has been solar evaporated and briefly kiln dried, is high in essential trace minerals as well as sodium chloride. No synthetic iodine or other chemicals have been added. As body chemistry should be kept balanced, excessive salt should be avoided.

Peanut Butter — Peanut butter is a rich source of protein, and when spread on whole wheat bread, provides a well-balanced protein. It is easily stored, and makes a nutritious as well as delicious addition to almost any meal. Most commercial peanut butter is hydrogenated (a process considered harmful to health by many medical experts) and contains other additives. "Deaf Smith" Brand Old Fashioned peanut butter is just pure sun-dried Valencia peanuts, famous for their taste.

Pressed Cooking oils — Unrefined, pressed cooking oils are oils which smell and taste like the grain or seed from which they were pressed. Refined oils, some unfortunately labeled with the misnomer "cold pressed", are usually light, clear, odorless products which have had much of the nutrient value stripped away. If the corn germ oil, olive oil, peanut oil, safflower oil, sesame oil, soy oil and wheat germ oil you use has the Arrowhead label, you know that it has not been hexane extracted, bleached, or otherwise denatured. Using good quality un-refined, pressed oils is equally as important as using good quality whole grain flours. Most unrefined oils should not be heated over 350 degrees F. For deep frying up to 400 degrees F, safflower oil should be used. Using a blend of several oils, such as safflower, soy, and peanut oils, provides a better balance of unsaturated fatty acids than does any single oil.

Dried Fruits — Dried apples, apricots, peaches and pears — along with dates, prunes and raisins, are excellent ways to satisfy a sweet tooth in a way that is beneficial to health. They make an excellent after-school snack, and are almost essential for camping and hiking trips. They can be eaten as is or soaked and added to breads, pancakes and dessert dishes as well as eaten as a fruit salad.

Sea Vegetables — Many essential minerals and vitamins are found in abundance in food from the sea. Sea vegetables such as dulse, nori, and wakame can be a nice addition to many dishes, especially soups. They come packaged dry in case you don't live close to the ocean. Soak the dried sea vegetables for about 15 minutes before inclusion in your recipe.

Apple Cider Vinegar — There is a lot of interest in the healthful properties of this product. But it should be made the old-fashioned way from apples which have been grown with natural methods. We know a fine man over in Virginia who does it just that way. We surely enjoy recommending people who try to do things right, especially when the final product tastes as good over vegetables or in oil and vinegar salad dressings as this one does.

Beverages — For those who like a hot cup to pick them up in the morning or during the day, there is a variety of herb teas which should include a taste or two for every pallate. These teas, such as chamomile, peppermint, rosehips, spearmint, comfrey, lemongrass and various blended flavors have beneficial effects in the body. A squeeze of lemon juice makes them even better. Several of these herb teas make a good iced tea.

You probably have some favorite fruit juices. Pure fruit juice is not only very good for you, when taken in moderation, but the taste of a glass full of ice cold tangy grape or apple juice on a hot day surely hits the spot. As people turn more to plenty of water, taken between meals, pure juices and herb teas, many of the health problems caused by some of the highly advertised drinks in this country will be reduced.

Sweeteners — Since we know that the human body is designed to handle the natural foods which were the common diet until just a few years ago, we can be sure that there is truth in the ample medical evidence that the refined sugars and flours which make up a huge portion of the food intake of this nation are having a disastrous effect, both in the individual lives of our people, and in society as a whole, as medical costs skyrocket. Within the concept of whole natural foods, honey, maple syrup, and molasses are popular, though these should be used with moderation.

THE IMPORTANCE OF A HIGH FIBER DIET:

WHEAT BRAN — Wheat bran can be added to any soup, casserole, bread, salad or dessert type recipe of your choice, either in the main recipe or perhaps as a garnish. Be sure to ask your natural foods store for Arrowhead wheat bran, however. In keeping with the quality standards of Arrowhead Mills, the Arrowhead label wheat bran comes only from wheat raised by natural methods and stored without fumigation. This is most important as pesticide residue or fumigants would tend to accumulate in the bran layers.

Special Note — For those who would like to begin their adventure into natural foods with a ready to cook "meal-in-a-bag", we recommend the exciting meal preparations from Earthwonder Farm, Blue Eye, Missouri, 65611. These nutritionally balanced one-pot meals, including grains, garnishings and seasonings, are also ideal for campers, hikers and anyone who would like to have it ready to put in the pot when they come home from work.

Note: Arrowhead Mills Wheat Flakes and Yellow Cornmeal make excellent extenders when added to your favorite food for your dog. Wheat Flakes should be cooked over low heat.

SPROUTING

In order to obtain the maximum benefit of the living foods called grains, beans and seeds, one can sprout them according to the following chart. Vitamin content is increased, as well as enzymes activated which will provide good health along with just a few other foods. It is important that the grains, beans, or seeds be cleaned extremely well. That is why Arrowhead Mills uses three cleaning processes before bagging.

A wide-mouth glass jar is suitable for sprouting. A tablespoon of seed in a pint jar covered with water for 12 hours or so gets you started. Then place a piece of cheesecloth or nylon netting over the mouth and secure it with a rubber band. You can then drain off the soaking water, rinse with warm rinse water, drain thoroughly, and leave jar tilted with mouth down. Room temperature and indirect light works fine. Rinse and drain each morning and evening — perhaps more often if humidity is extremely low.

After the sprouts have reached the desired length, place in direct sunlight for a few hours to develop chlorophyll, rinse with cold water, drain and store, tightly covered in refrigerator. Eat them as soon as possible, preferably within two or three days. Sprout only enough seeds for this usage, and you can be starting a new batch every day or so. Be sure seeds are obtained from a reputable company and have not been treated. Do not eat potato sprouts as they are toxic. Sprouting is a great activity for children. Our daughter, Cindy, won her school's science contest when she was 10 years old with her "Sprouting for Food" project. You will be surprised at how much life can come from these little seeds. Following are the sprouting times and the optimum length of sprout in inches for each of the seeds most often sprouted for food:

SPROUTING CHART

Seeds	Sprouting time in days	Optimum length of sprout in inches
Alfalfa	4 to 5	1 to 2
Garbanzo beans	3 to 4	3/4 to 1
Lentils	2 to 3	length of seed
Mung beans	3 to 4	1 to 1—1/2
Rye	2	length of seed
Wheat	2	length of seed
Soybeans*	3 to 4	1/2 to 3/4

*While most of the above seeds are very easy to sprout correctly, soybeans become moldy very easily. It is essential to rinse them very thoroughly each time, drain them well, and not crowd them in jar. Soybeans sprouts and Garbanzo sprouts are best cooked as they are still large and tough.

Sprouts can be added to salads, soups, casseroles, sandwiches — or munched on just as is. They can be cooked with vegetables or eggs, or ground and used in bread recipes. They will quicken the leavening action of yeast breads and help unleavened breads rise. Most importantly, they will improve the nutrition of any meal. If a person had to survive a year on, say, 300 lbs. of food — grains, beans and seeds for spouting would make up most of the supply list for the survival. Isn't it nice that they taste good, too? Alfalfa sprouts are great in salads and sandwiches. The heavier bean sprouts are really tasty when sauteed with onions and other vegetables. Best wishes in your sprouting adventure.

Yogurt & Sourdough Recipes

YOGURT

The best use of milk, whether it be from the cow or goat, is to make it into yogurt, except, of course, for an infant that cannot receive enough milk at its mother's breast. Yogurt is easily digestible, and the beneficial bacteria in it multiply at body temperature, producing B vitamins and overcoming many mild stomach upsets. Yogurt is especially important to restore intestinal flora after use of antibiotics. It can be eaten plain or with fruit or honey. It can be used in place of sour cream dressing for many uses. Granola and yogurt go well together.

How to make your own yogurt:

    1 quart fresh milk
    3 tablespoons or more of yogurt

Be sure all utensils are scalded. Heat milk to scalding. Cool to lukewarm. Blend in a little non-instant milk powder if thicker yogurt is desired (optional). Stir yogurt into the lukewarm milk. Pour the mixture into scalded glasses or jars. Place jars in large pan of warm water. Maintain at about 110 degrees for 3 to 5 hours until the new yogurt thickens. Refrigerate until used.

SOURDOUGH BREAD

Sourdough bread takes perhaps twice as long to rise as yeast dough, but it is actually easier to make as well as very tasty, depending on the quality of the starter. Sourdough also makes great rolls and pancakes. Many campers have taken some starter along and had a good breakfast working for them through the night.

How to make your own sourdough starter:

    1/2 package dry yeast
    1 cup lukewarm water
    1 cup whole wheat pastry flour

Dissolve yeast in water and let sit for 15 minutes. Slowly add the flour and mix well. Place in scalded jar. Let sit at room temperature for several days, until fermented and bubbly. Stir well and refrigerate. Starter is now ready to feed for making bread. It is best to feed starter every week or so, using an equivalent amount. If the starter ferments longer and liquid separates, just stir it back in, feed it and use it.

Feeding your sourdough starter:

> 1 cup of starter
> 2 cups warm water
> 2 cups whole wheat pastry flour

Always use earthenware bowl to let starter rise in. Do not use metal. Beat all the ingredients together with a fork. Remove fork. Let sit overnight. Return 1 cup of the starter to the refrigerator. This leaves about three cups of starter to use — enough for some pancakes and two loaves of bread (see sourdough bread and pancake recipes).

TAKE SOURDOUGH TO CAMP

> 1 cup sourdough starter
> Whole wheat flour — take plenty

Knead enough flour into the starter to make a soft dough. Sprinkle the dough with more flour. Carry the dough in a plastic bag containing a cup of dry flour. Keep the bag tightly closed. Sourdough starter must be mixed with flour because it can only be stored in liquid form in glass or ceramic containers, which are too heavy and inconvenient for camping. The starter will keep a week or more. Keep the starter fresh by feeding and using it once a week or more.

To use this starter: Place the soft dough starter in a bowl. Add 2 to 4 cups of warm water and 2 to 4 cups of flour. Set the bowl in a warm place 3 to 4

hours or overnight (near a warm fire in the winter).
Now the starter is ready to use in any sourdough
recipe.

SOURDOUGH ON A STICK

Sourdough bread dough —
> *Or thick sourdough pancake batter with enough*
>   *flour added to make a soft dough*
> *Or use dough made from plain pancake batter*
>   *using less liquid than called for.*

green sticks, peeled
hot coals from camp fire

>— Prepare the dough. Roll pieces of dough into
long skinny sausages about 1/4 inch thick. Wet
the green stick and heat it over the coals. Wrap
the dough around the warmed stick. Hold the
dough over the hot coals until baked, turning to
prevent burning. Dip the dough in a mixture of
melted honey, butter, and cinnamon before baking if desired.

SOURDOUGH PANCAKES
Serves 4

Feed your starter an extra amount the night before.

2 cups sourdough starter, the consistency of a heavy
pancake batter
1/2 cup warm water
2 tablespoons raw honey
2 teaspoons sea salt
2 teaspoons low-sodium baking powder
2 eggs
4 tablespoons unrefined oil

>— Dissolve the honey and salt in the warm water.
Add the baking powder, then stir this mixture
into the starter. Beat in the eggs and oil with a
spoon until the mixture is smooth. Bake on a
medium hot, oiled griddle.

PRIMITIVE BREAD

Sourdough bread dough
plenty of green leaves (maple, aspen, bay, magnolia,
*   birch, etc.)*
hot coals

Allow the bread dough to rise once. Pat the
dough into a 1/2 inch thick cake. Place the
dough on several thicknesses of leaves. Scrape
coals and ashes to one side. Place the leaves and
dough on the hot fire base. Cover the dough
well with more green leaves. Then cover with
ashes, followed by a layer of hot coals. Let the
bread bake under the ashes and coals about 10
to 15 minutes. Test after 10 minutes by poking
the bread with a long, thin twig. If it comes out
clean, the bread is done.

SOURDOUGH BATTER BREAD

Yield: 1 loaf

2 cups sourdough starter
1 tablespoon raw honey
1 tablespoon unrefined oil
1 teaspoon sea salt
2 tablespoons soy flour
3 to 4 cups whole flour

Feed the starter the night before. Stir all ingredients together except the flours. Mix dry
ingredients and slowly beat into the batter.
Beat for 5 minutes. Pour batter into a greased
9 x 5 inch loaf pan. Let rise until batter is just
over rim of pan. Bake 50 minutes at 350 degrees.

SOURDOUGH BREAD

Yield: 2 loaves

1 cup sourdough starter
2 cups warm water
1 to 4 tablespoons raw honey
1 tablespoon sea salt
1/2 cup unrefined oil
6 cups whole wheat flour

Feed your starter the night before. Let it sit overnight. Use a large ceramic or crock bowl. Beat all the ingredients except the flour together. Add the flour. Mix well, by hand if necessary. Cover the dough and let it rise 3 to 4 hours or until doubled. In summer it may take less time. Shape the dough into 2 loaves, kneading a little as you shape them. Place in oiled loaf pans. Let rise 1 to 2 hours until doubled. The bread will rise a little more while cooking. Bake 30 to 40 minutes at 350 degrees. Turn out on a rack to cool.

General Cooking Instructions

A Brief Note About The Following Recipe Ideas:

The foods used have been combined for maximum. protein effectiveness, over-all nutrition, ease of preparation, and taste. These recipe ideas are designed for camp cooks, cuisine chefs who want to get into natural foods, mothers who want to prepare delicious food in just a few minutes, and anybody else who would like to get away from the plastic world of highly processed, de-natured foods. All of us here at Arrowhead Mills hope that these ideas will increase your eating enjoyment, improve your health, and help your budget. You might be surprised at the many ways in which your life can be improved by a visit to your nearest natural foods store. Our bodies were created by God to function well on the foods that He created — natural foods. Please use your own skills to modify, substitute and improve as you go along in the exciting world of natural foods cookery.

(P. S. — Over the past four decades, I have enjoyed approximately 400 days and nights of camping. During this time, I have built stone ovens in the mountains and used easily carried reflector ovens on the canoe trails. The more complicated recipes which follow can be done in the wilds. However, it would be best to save them for the kitchen, and use the simple ones in the woods.)

How To Saute Vegetables —

Heat a heavy pan to moderate heat. Add a good quality unrefined oil (see product information section on oils) to coat the bottom of the pan. Add the chopped vegetables (or grain) immediately and stir lightly with a wooden spoon or spatula. After the vegetables have heated through, reduce heat and let the vegetables cook in their own juices until tender. Start with tougher ones first, adding those which are more tender. This is a highly recommended method of cooking, both for taste and nutrition. In most of the dishes, which require subsequent simmering, you can saute in a pot large and deep enough to add your water, and save cleaning an extra utensil. In nearly any soup as well as grain and vegetable dishes, sautéing in a good unrefined oil prior to simmering locks in taste and tenderness as well as the extra nutrition of the oil.

How To Add Water —

Doesn't that sound ridiculous? I said to my wife, Margie, who is a co-author of the best selling Deaf Smith Country Cookbook, "Anybody knows to add enough water to keep something from burning." She answered, "Good cooks want to know how much water to start with". Since she knows how much I don't know about cooking, I am going to compromise, do what she says, and put approximate amounts of water required to cook the various things, and cooking times therefor. But I still think you could figure it out on your own. Even I generally hit it about right out on a camp.

Cooking Whole Grains, Flakes, Cereals & Beans, How To —

Per 1 cup of dry	Add Water	Cover and simmer about
Barley	2½ cups	60 minutes
Millet	3½ cups	30 minutes
Oat flakes	3 cups	30 minutes
Rice, short grain	2½ cups	50 minutes
medium grain	2 cups	50 minutes
long grain	1½ cups	45 minutes
flaked	2 cups	20 minutes
Rye	2½ cups	60 minutes
flaked	2 cups	20 minutes
Wheat	2½ cups	60 minutes
flaked	2 cups	20 minutes
cracked	3 cups	20 minutes

Per 1 cup of dry	Add Water	Cover & Simmer
Chick-peas (soak overnight)	4 cups	2 - 3 hours
Lentils	3 cups	1 hour
Pinto Beans	3 cups	2 - 3 hours
Soybeans (soak overnight)	4 cups	3 - 4 hours
Soybeans, flaked	2 cups	1 - 2 hours
Split Peas	3 cups	45 minutes

Note — The above approximations, which will vary with altitude and several other factors, are for cooking up all the free water. For soups, more water and longer simmering times are required. . .the more people who drop in unexpectedly, the more water. Excess water should never be poured off, as it contains vitamins and minerals from the food cooked in it. If there is an excess, you might save it for soup stock.

BREAKFASTS

SCRAMBLED EGGS WITH SPROUTS
SERVES 4-6

> 8 to 10 eggs
> 1/2 cup milk
> 4 green onions, including tops, finely chopped
> 1 teaspoon sea salt or
>   1 tablespoon tamari soy sauce
> 1 cup mung bean sprouts or alfalfa sprouts
> 1 tablespoon of unrefined oil

Beat the eggs with the milk and seasonings. Stir in the sprouts. Heat a large skillet on medium heat. Add the oil. Then add the beaten egg mixture. Cook, stirring often, until the eggs are barely set. Season to taste.

TOAST AND EGGS
SERVES 6

> 6 eggs
> 6 slices whole wheat bread
> 2 tablespoons unrefined oil

Remove a 3 inch diameter center from each piece of bread. Oil hot griddle. Toast bread on one side. Flip bread over (keep griddle oiled) and break an egg carefully into the hole in each piece of toast. Season to taste. (Toast the center portions for the children to snack on while breakfast is cooking.)

BUCKWHEAT MUSH
SERVES 4

> 2/3 cup buckwheat groats
> 2/3 cup oat flakes
> 1/2 cup non-instant dry milk powder

1/2 cup raisins
4 cups boiling water

Combine the buckwheat groats and oats. Add
the dry milk and raisins. Pour boiling water
over all and bring mixture to a very low simmer. Cover and simmer 10 to 15 minutes or
until the grains are softened. Add honey to
taste and serve.

BULGHUR BREAKFAST
SERVES 8

1-1/2 cups bulghur-soy grits
1/2 teaspoon sea salt
4 cups boiling water
1/2 cup wheat germ
1/4 cup sesame seeds
1/4 cup chopped almonds

Stir grits and salt into the water. Reduce heat,
cover, and simmer for 10 to 15 minutes until
nearly tender. Add other ingredients and simmer a few more minutes. Add chopped dried
apples with other ingredients if you wish. Top
with a little honey.

GRANDMA'S COUNTRY MUSH
SERVES 4 - 6

6 cups boiling water
1 cup currants
1/4 teaspoon sea salt or salt to taste
2 cups flaked rye, or other flaked grain

Add all ingredients to the water. Cover and simmer on low heat about 30 minutes, stirring occasionally.

GRANOLA, HOMEMADE STYLE

> 5 cups mixed wheat, rye and oat flakes
> 1 to 2 cups mixture of seeds and/or chopped nuts
> 1/2 cup unrefined oil
> 1/4 to 1/2 cup raw honey, molasses or maple syrup
> 5 cups wheat flakes
> 2 cups raisins or chopped dried fruits

Stir first 5 cups of flakes, seeds or nuts, oil and sweetener together. Spread thin on cookie sheets. Bake 2 to 4 minutes in a hot 400 degree oven till lightly toasted. Stir into remaining flakes and fruit to cool and keep from lumping. Cool completely and store in air tight containers.

CAMPER'S BREAKFAST

> brown rice, whole grain wheat, or
>   other whole grains
> pinch of sea salt
> boiling water
> thermos

Use a thermos or heavy sauce pan with a heavy, tight-fitting lid. Fill thermos 1/3 full of whole grain. Add a pinch of salt. Fill the remainder of the thermos with boiling water. Seal immediately and let sit overnight. The grain will be ready for breakfast. You can't ask for an easier breakfast than that. Grain may be eaten cold or reheated.

FLAKES AND FRUIT
SERVES 8

> 3 tablespoons unrefined oil
> 2 cups flaked wheat, rye, triticale
>   or rice (or mixture)
> 1/2 teaspoon sea salt
> 5 to 6 cups boiling water

> 1/4 cup soy flour
> 1/2 cup raisins, chopped dates,
>   or other chopped dried fruits

><> Saute the flakes in oil.   Add water and salt.
Cover and simmer until tender, about 15 minutes. Stir in soy flour and fruit. Simmer a few
more minutes.

SPROUTED WHEAT CEREAL
SERVES 8

> 3 cups sprouted wheat (see sprout chart)
> 2 tablespoons raw honey
> 1/2 cup chopped dried fruit

><> Steam sprouted wheat and dried fruit in a little
water until both are tender. Add honey if desired.

RYE FLAKE CEREAL
SERVES 4

> 1 cup rye flakes
> 1/2 teaspoon sea salt
> 4 cups boiling water
> 1/2 cup oat flakes
> 1/4 cup soy flour
> 1/2 cup raisins

><> Add rye flakes and salt to the water. Reduce
heat, cover and simmer 10 minutes. Mix oat
flakes and soy flour and add to the rye. Cover
and simmer another 15 minutes. Add raisins
and a little honey to taste.

WHEAT FLAKE CEREAL
SERVES 4

> 1 tablespoon unrefined oil
> 1 cup wheat flakes or other flaked grain
> 3 cups boiling water
> 1/4 teaspoon sea salt

Saute flakes in oil until golden brown. Add water and salt. Cover and simmer for 30 minutes, stirring occasionally. Serve with roasted seeds or nuts and raisins.

WHEAT AND SESAME CEREAL
SERVES 4

> 1 tablespoon unrefined oil
> 1 cup cracked wheat or bulghur
> 1/4 cup sesame seeds
> 1/4 cup wheat germ
> 1/4 cup unsweetened coconut
> 3 cups water
> Optional: 1/2 teaspoon sea salt, dried fruits,
> chopped nuts.

Heat a heavy pan. Add the oil and the cracked wheat, sesame seeds, wheat germ, and coconut. Saute until light brown. Add the water, and salt and dried fruits if desired. Cover and steam about 25 minutes, until the cracked wheat is fluffy. Add nuts to taste. Serve with milk and honey.

WHOLE GRAIN FLOUR CEREAL
SERVES 6

> 4 cups boiling water
> 1-1/2 teaspoons sea salt
> 1-1/2 cups whole wheat flour, or
> other whole grain flour

1/2 cup raisins or chopped dried fruit
raw honey
milk or cream

Add water to flour gradually, beating to prevent
lumping. Add salt and fruit. Cover and simmer,
stirring occasionally, for 10 to 15 minutes. Serve
with honey and milk.

PEANUT BUTTER FLAPJACKS

SERVES 4 - 6

2 cups whole wheat pastry flour
1/2 teaspoon sea salt
1 egg, slightly beaten
2 cups milk
2 tablespoons pure maple syrup or honey
2 tablespoons unrefined oil
1 tablespoon yeast dissolved in
    1/4 cup warm water
1/4 cup old fashioned peanut butter

Mix the flour and salt. Mix the egg, milk, syrup,
oil and dissolved yeast. Gradually stir liquids
into the peanut butter until smooth. Add this
to the flour mixture and stir just until moistened. Let the batter sit for 15 minutes. Batter
will be thin. Bake on hot griddle until browned
on both sides.

RYE CORNMEAL PANCAKES

SERVES 4 - 6

2 eggs, beaten
6 tablespoons molasses
1 cup milk
1 cup rye flour
1 cup cornmeal
1/2 teaspoon sea salt

Blend eggs, molasses and milk. Mix remaining

ingredients and stir into liquid. Add more rye
flour if necessary to make the batter stiff. Drop
by spoonfuls onto a heated oiled frypan. Brown
lightly on both sides.

QUICK SOY PANCAKES
SERVES 8

> 1-1/2 cups soy flour
> 1/2 cup stone-ground corn meal
> 2 cups whole wheat flour
> 2 tablespoons low-sodium baking powder
> 1/2 teaspoon sea salt
> 2 cups milk
> 5 eggs
> 1/3 cup raw honey

Mix the dry ingredients. Beat the liquid ingredients together and stir the flour mixture into the
liquid. Refrigerate overnight. Add about 2 cups
warm water in the morning and bake on a medium-hot, oiled griddle.

TRAVELING PANCAKE MIX

YIELD: 3 breakfasts for 4 people

> 6 cups whole wheat flour
> 1 cup non-instant milk powder
> 2 tablespoons low-sodium baking powder
> 1 tablespoon sea salt

Mix all ingredients together. Carry in a tightly
closed half-gallon container. When ready to use,
add 2 cups water, 2 eggs, and 2 tablespoons unrefined oil to each 2-1/3 cups of the dry mix. If
you don't carry eggs, increase the amount of oil
to 3 or 4 tablespoons.

QUICK WHOLE WHEAT PANCAKES
SERVES 4

>   2 cups whole wheat flour
>   1 teaspoon sea salt
>   2 teaspoons low-sodium baking powder
>   2 cups milk
>   2 eggs, beaten well
>   2 tablespoons unrefined oil

Mix the dry ingredients together. Mix the liquid ingredients and add to the dry ingredients. Stir, adding a little water if necessary to get proper consistency. Bake on a medium-heat, oiled griddle or heavy skillet.

FAST YEAST PANCAKES
SERVES 6

>   3 cups milk
>   3 eggs, beaten
>   3 tablespoons unrefined oil
>   3 tablespoons raw honey
>   4 tablespoons active dry yeast
>   1 cup whole wheat flour
>   1 cup triticale flour
>   1 cup soy flour
>   1 teaspoon sea salt

Mix and warm the liquids. Mix the dry ingredients together. Add the liquid mixture to the flour mixture and beat 2 minutes. Let the batter sit 5 minutes. Bake on a medium-hot, oiled griddle.

PANCAKE VARIATIONS:

- Liquids used may be fruit juices, water, milk, buttermilk, or yogurt.

- Any flour or meal may be substituted for all or part of the flour called for.

- Chopped fresh fruit or soaked dried fruits — or sprouts — may be added to batter.

- Pancakes may serve for any course from breakfast to dessert by varying the sauces from sweet to creamed to cheese sauce. Pancakes make an excellent quick bread on a camping trip, and are good with peanut butter on them for a quick energy mid-afternoon snack.

SALADS

TABOOLIE
SERVES 8

> 2 cups cracked wheat cereal
> 1 cup chopped parsley
> 1/2 cup chopped onions
> 2 tomatoes, chopped
> 1/2 to 1 cup lemon juice
> 1/2 to 1 cup unrefined safflower oil
> salt and pepper to taste

>⤜ Soak the cracked wheat in 1 cup warm water for an hour or so. Add other ingredients and toss together. Chill before serving. Don't miss this taste treat.

STUFFED TOMATO SALAD
SERVES 6

> 6 large tomatoes
> 2 cups cooked garbanzas
> 4 tablespoons mungbean sprouts
> 4 tablespoons unrefined oil
> 2 tablespoons dulse
> 2 tablespoons roasted soy flour
> 2 tablespoons grated onion

>⤜ Scoop out tomatoes. Mix remaining ingredients. Fill tomato cavities. Chill Serve on lettuce or raw spinach leaves.

TOSSED SALADS

>⤜ Wash your greens and vegetables quickly in cold water and dry with paper towel. Chill if not used immediately. Tear the greens and chop other crisp vegetables. Toss immediately in enough

unrefined oil to coat the cut edges. Only then add your chopped wet vegetables, such as tomatoes, and your choice of dressing. This procedure will prevent vitamin loss and will keep the salad crisp.

Use all kinds of colorful crisp vegetables to add nutrients and beauty to your salads. Rely heavily on sprouts, as growing your own sprouts guarantees you cheap, fresh, unsprayed greens all the year around. They add great variety in taste and texture and abundant vitamins. Raw vegetables are an essential part of a good diet.

CARROT, CABBAGE, AND RAISIN SALAD

1 cup finely shredded cabbage
3 cups grated carrots
1/2 cup raisins
1/2 cup mayonnaise
1/2 teaspoon sea salt
1 teaspoon raw honey
2 teaspoons lemon juice

Mix the vegetables and raisins. Mix the mayonnaise, salt, honey, and lemon juice. Stir all together well.

DRIED FRUIT SALAD
SERVES 6

4 ounces of dried apples
12 ounces of mixed, dried fruit
juice of one large lemon
1/4 cup raw honey

Chop fruit into small bite sizes. Toss with lemon juice and then honey to coat each piece. Cover and refrigerate or keep in a cool place till moist.

JERUSALEM ARTICHOKE SALAD
SERVES 4

> *5 to 6 Jerusalem artichokes, grated*
> *2 carrots, grated*
> *3 stalks of celery, strung and chopped fine*
> *1/3 cup chopped parsley*
> *homemade mayonnaise or other dressing*
> *Garnish: carrot curls and black olives*

Wash and grate or chop the vegetables. Mix lightly with desired dressing. Serve on a lettuce leaf. Garnish individual plates or the salad bowl before serving. Other raw vegetables may be added. If desired, add a little spicy or hot sauce or seasoned sea salt to the mayonnaise.

MUNGBEAN SLAW
SERVES 6

> *2 cups mungbean sprouts*
> *2 cups shredded cabbage*
> *2 tablespoons dulse*
> *1 small onion, grated*
> *1/2 cup green pepper, chopped*
> *2 tablespoons unrefined oil*

Toss vegetables with the oil. Then add dulse and a favorite dressing.

LENTIL SALAD
SERVES 8

> *2 cups lentils, rinsed*
> *6 cups boiling water*
> *1/2 cup apple cider vinegar*
> *1/2 cup unrefined safflower oil*
> *minced garlic*
> *sea salt or tamari soy sauce*
> *paprika*

➤ Add lentils to water and cook about 30 minutes or until tender. Drain and cool. Mix oil and vinegar and stir lightly into lentils. Season with garlic, salt, and paprika. Refrigerate and serve chilled with tomatoes and lettuce or alfalfa sprouts.

HOT RICE SALAD
SERVES 6

> 2 cups hot, cooked rice
> 1 onion, chopped
> 1 tablespoon lemon juice
> 1/4 cup unrefined olive oil
> sea salt, pepper, and oregano to taste

➤ Blend the oil and lemon juice and add to rice and chopped onion. Season to taste.

MARINATED MUSHROOMS
YIELD: 3 CUPS

> 1/2 pound mushrooms, with stems
> 1/4 teaspoon sea salt or 1 teaspoon tamari soy sauce
> 1/2 teaspoon oregano
> 3 tablespoons lemon juice
> 1/2 cup unrefined olive oil

➤ Rinse and wipe the mushrooms and slice them evenly. Mix the salt or tamari, oregano, lemon juice, and olive oil. Add to the mushrooms. Allow to stand at room temperature 2 to 3 hours or overnight.

RICE AND FRUIT SALAD
SERVES 6

> *2 cups cooked brown rice*
> *1/2 cup almonds, slivered*
> *1/2 cup mayonnaise or yogurt*
> *1 orange, peeled and cubed*
> *1/2 cup grapes, seeded and halved*

✂ Chill all the ingredients thoroughly. Then mix
them lightly and serve at once on lettuce.

SLAW

> *1 cabbage, shredded*
> *1 carrot, grated*
> *1 bell pepper, chopped fine*

✂ Fold the vegetables into the dressing.

YOGURT DRESSING FOR SLAW
YIELD: 1-1-1/2 CUPS

> *1 cup yogurt*
> *1/2 cup mayonnaise*
> *2 tablespoons lemon juice*
> *1/8 teaspoon sea salt*
> *2 tablespoons raw honey*

✂ Mix all the ingredients well.

SPINACH & EGG SALAD
SERVES 6

> *1 pound raw spinach, washed and stems*
>   *removed*
> *1 tablespoon unrefined oil*
> *1 large onion, chopped*
> *1 tomato, chopped*

➤ Toss spinach with the oil. Add other ingredients and toss with dressing of unrefined safflower oil, lemon juice and garlic. For WATERCRESS SALAD: If you happen to be near a stream where watercress grows, you will enjoy substituting it for or mixing it with the spinach in this salad or greens of any other salad.

SOYBEAN SALAD

SERVES 6

>   *3 cups cooked soy flakes*
>   *juice of 1 lime*
>   *1 bell pepper, chopped*
>   *1 onion, chopped*
>   *1 tomato, chopped*

➤ Toss flakes, juice, and vegetables and serve with tahini dressing.

SPROUT & GROW SALAD

>   *2 cups alfalfa sprouts*
>   *3 tomatoes, chopped*
>   *2 bell peppers, diced*
>   *2 onions, chopped*

➤ Toss lightly with oil and vinegar dressing. Serve immediately.

SPROUT & VEGETABLE SALAD

>   *2 cups mingbean sprouts or alfalfa sprouts*
>   *5 radishes, sliced*
>   *1 cucumber, sliced*
>   *1 bell pepper, diced*
>   *2 tablespoons unrefined oil*

➤ Mix sprouts and vegetables together. Toss with oil. Chill and serve with Tahini Dressing.

ARROWHEAD'S MAKE-YOUR-OWN MAYONNAISE

YIELD: 1 cup
        1 egg
        2 tablespoons lemon juice or vinegar
        1/4 cup unrefined oil
        1/2 to 1 teaspoon dry mustard
        3/4 teaspoon sea salt
        1/4 teaspoon white pepper
        3/4 cup unrefined oil

Combine egg, lemon juice, 1/4 cup oil, dry mustard, sea salt, and pepper in electric blender jar. Cover and blend at low speed until mixed. Increase speed to high, uncover or remove center cap, and add remaining oil in a thin, slow, steady stream. Blend until all the oil is added and mayonnaise is smooth and creamy. If necessary, turn motor off and stir occasionally. Always replace cover before turning motor back on. Keep mayonnaise refrigerated, and use within 7 to 10 days.

The five following recipes were contributed by The Good Food People, Inc. of Austin, Texas (see Source list) Hoot Shaw and the other Good Food People know the value of fresh raw vegetables.

POTATO SALAD

        new potatoes, unpeeled
        dill pickles, chopped
        celery, chopped
        green onions and chives, chopped
        olives, chopped
        Seasonings: fresh dill weed, fresh parsley,
            1/2 teaspoon dry mustard, 1 teaspoon kelp
            powder, 1/2 teaspoon paprika, sea salt to taste.
            Yogurt or mayonnaise

Cut potatoes into chunks and boil until tender. Drain and cool. Add chopped vegetables. Then add seasonings and mix together with enough yogurt or mayonnaise to make a light, creamy sauce.

WONDERFUL SALAD

fresh spinach and lettuce
favorite sprouts
chopped celery
chopped green onions
sliced cucumbers
fresh green peas
pieces of broccoli tops
tomatoes
raw sunflower seeds
grated cheese

➤ Combine all ingredients. For a super dressing, toss in a mellow blend of mashed avocados and lemon juice.

SEA VEGETABLE SALAD

romaine lettuce
chopped green onions
chopped celery
sliced avocado
alfalfa sprouts
dulse, or favorite sea vegetable
kelp powder to taste

➤ Mix in all ingredients to taste and sprinkle with lemon juice.

STUFFED TOMATOES

large ripe tomatoes
mayonnaise
mashed avocado
alfalfa sprouts
chopped green onions

➤ Remove pulp from the tomatoes. Drain the juice and mix pulp with remaining ingredients, adding kelp powder and lemon juice to taste. Stir well and stuff into tomato shells. Top with a dash of paprika and a cauliflowerette.

DRESSINGS

BUTTERMILK SALAD DRESSING

2 cups buttermilk
3/4 cup cottage cheese
1/4 cup cider vinegar
1 tablespoon Italian herbs

Beat together and store in a covered jar in refrigerator.

GREEN GODDESS YOGURT DRESSING

YIELD: 1 CUP

1/2 cup yogurt
1 ripe avocado or 1/2 cup cooked asparagus, drained, or 1/2 cucumber
1 teaspoon sea salt
1 small clove garlic, chopped
1 tablespoon lime juice
Optional: chopped chives, parsley, or mint
1 teaspoon chili powder

Mash or blend all the ingredients together. Chill.

PEANUT BUTTER SALAD DRESSING

YIELD: 1 CUP

2 tablespoons old fashioned peanut butter
2 tablespoons water
2 tablespoons cider vinegar
4 tablespoons unrefined oil
2 tablespoons tamari soy sauce

Blend all the ingredients well in a blender.

QUICK TAMARI ORANGE SALAD DRESSING
YIELD: 1/2 CUP

> juice of one orange
> 2 tablespoons unrefined olive oil
> 3 tablespoons tamari soy sauce

>—Pour all the ingredients in a jar and shake well.

TOMATO DRESSING
YIELD: 1 CUP

> 1/2 cup tomato juice
> 1/2 cup yogurt
> 1 teaspoon lemon juice

>—Mix well. Chill.

PAUL'S SALAD DRESSING
YIELD: 1 1/2 CUPS

> 3/4 cup unrefined sesame oil
> juice of 1 orange
> 1 tablespoon tamari soy sauce
> 1 tablespoon tahini

>—Blend all ingredients together in a blender or beat well. Add 1 tablespoon water if needed to prevent separation.

SOUPS

BARLEY SOUP
SERVES 8

    2 tablespoons unrefined oil
    1-1/2 cups pearled barley
    2 onions, chopped
    2 stalks celery, chopped
    4 cups water
    1 cup sliced mushrooms
    1/4 cup chopped parsley

Saute barley, onions and celery for 5 minutes. Add water and bring to a boil. Simmer for an hour or so. Saute mushrooms and add to soup. Season to taste with tamari or sea salt. Garnish with parsley.

BEAN SOUP

YIELD: 6 CUPS

    4 cups cooked black beans, pinto beans, or soy
        beans and thick juice from cooking
    2 cups water or stock
    2 tablespoons lime juice
    4 teaspoons unrefined oil
    2 small onions, finely chopped
    2 teaspoons sea salt
    1 to 2 teaspoons sea salt
    Garnish: 6 tablespoons yogurt mixed with
        1/2 teaspoon chili powder

Simmer all ingredients until thick. Garnish just before serving

BEAN AND FLAKE SOUP

SERVES 3 or 4

    2 tablespoons unrefined oil
    1 small bunch green onions and tops, chopped
    2 cloves garlic, finely chopped
    1 cup cooked pinto bean flakes or mashed
        cooked pinto beans or other beans

1 cup cooked rice grain flakes or other grain
     flakes or cooked whole grains
1 cup juice from cooking bean flakes, or water
1 tablespoon tamari soy sauce
1 cup fresh milk
1/4 teaspoon sweet red pepper or
     1/8 teaspoon cayenne pepper
Garnish: homemade yogurt

Heat a large saucepan. Add the oil, onions and garlic and saute. Add the flakes and juice and simmer 2 minutes, stirring constantly. Add the soy sauce, milk and other seasonings and just heat through. Garnish with yogurt. Pinto Soup is a southwestern favorite — hearty and spicy.

SPANISH BEAN SOUP
SERVES 8

2 cups dry pinto beans
6 cups boiling water
2 teaspoons chili powder
2 tablespoons unrefined oil
2 cloves garlic, chopped
2 onions, chopped
1 green papper, chopped

Add pintos to the water. Cover and cook until almost tender, 2 to 3 hours. Add chili powder. Saute remaining ingredients in the oil and add. Simmer until everything is tender.

BEET AND CARROT SOUP
SERVES 6

1/4 cup unrefined oil
2 beets, diced
2 carrots, diced
1/2 cabbage, shredded
6 cups water
juice of one lemon

>—— Saute diced beets and carrots in the oil for 5 minutes. Add cabbage and saute for 20 minutes more. Add water and lemon juice and simmer until tender. Season with sea salt and herbs.

CELERY SOUP

SERVES 4

> 1 cup chopped celery
> 1/2 cup chopped onion
> 1/2 cup chopped carrots
> 3 sprigs parsley
> 2 tablespoons soy flour made into paste with
>   1/4 cup water
> 1/4 cup tamari soy sauce
> 4 cups water

>—— Mix all ingredients. Simmer 30 minutes.

FRESH CORN SOUP

SERVES 4 to 6

> 3 ears of corn
> 2 onions, chopped
> 3 cups water
> 1 tablespoon arrowroot powder, mixed in
>   1/4 cup water
> 1/4 teaspoon sea salt
> 1 teaspoon sea salt
> Garnish: minced scallions

>—— Scrape kernels off the cob. Bring the water to a boil. Add the corn and onions and simmer for 15 minutes. Add the salt and arrowroot and simmer 5 minutes more. Add salt to taste, and simmer for a few more minutes. Garnish with minced scallions.

GARBANZO GOULASH (CHICKPEAS)
SERVES 8

> 1-1/2 cups dry chickpeas, soaked overnight
> *6 cups water*
> *3 onions, chopped*
> *5 stalks celery, chopped*
> *3 tablespoons sesame butter*
> *2 tablespoons unrefined sesame oil*
> *1/4 cup whole wheat flour or cornmeal*

Soak chickpeas overnight. Next day cook in 6 cups water 2 to 3 hours. Add remaining ingredients. Simmer another 15 minutes or until tender. Season to taste with tamari and herbs.

JERUSALEM ARTICHOKE SOUP
SERVES 4

> *4 tablespoons unrefined oil*
> *1 pound Jerusalem artichokes, sliced thin*
> *2 onions, sliced thin*
> *2 cups hot water or vegetable stock*
> *1/2 teaspoon sea salt or to taste*
> *2 cups hot milk*
> *1/8 teaspoon nutmeg*

Heat a large saucepan. Add the oil, Jerusalem artichokes, and onions. Cover and saute on low heat, stirring often until vegetables are almost tender. Add the water or stock and salt. Cover and simmer until vegetables are soft. Mash the vegetables or blend in a blender. Add the hot milk and nutmeg. Heat through. Jerusalem artichokes are mild and sweet. They make a delicate creamy soup.

MILLET STEW
SERVES 8

> 7 cups boiling water
> 2 cups hulled millet
> 2 potatoes, diced
> 2 carrots, diced
> one onion, chopped

Add all ingredients to water. Cover and simmer until tender, about 30 minutes. Add tamari soy sauce and herbs to taste.

FRENCH ONION SOUP
YIELD: 4 CUPS

> 2 tablespoons unrefined corn germ oil
> 2 large onions, thinly sliced
> 1 tablespoon whole wheat flour
> 4 cups hot tamari broth or vegetable stock
> sea salt
> Garnish: toasted croutons, grated cheese

Heat a large saucepan. Add the oil and onions and saute until tender and golden brown. Add the flour and cook over low heat for about 2 minutes, stirring constantly. Add the hot broth and simmer 5 to 10 minutes. Season to taste with sea salt. Serve hot with the garnish.

POTATO SOUP
SERVES 6

> 3 large potatoes, diced
> 1 onion, chopped
> 8 cups water
> 2 tablespoons soy flour
> 2 tablespoons whole wheat flour
> 1/4 cup tamari

✄ Boil potatoes and onions till tender. Make paste with the flours and water and add. Stir in other ingredients and cook till thick. Season and garnish to taste with herbs and sesame seeds.

SOUP OF THE DAY

> *green peppers, chopped*
> *tomatoes chopped*
> *onions, chopped*
> *garlic, minced*
> *unrefined olive oil*
> *fresh vegetables — corn, squash, celery,*
> *cabbage, carrots, green beans, peas,*
> *shredded lettuce, potatoes, wild*
> *greens, etc.*
> *grains and beans — cooked soybeans, pinto*
> *beans, barley, rice, lentils, millet, etc.*

✄ Cook the first four ingredients down into a thick sauce. Add oil and your favorite combination of fresh vegetables and cooked grains. Cover with water. Simmer till done. Season to taste with herbs and sea salt.

SPLIT PEA OR LENTIL SOUP
SERVES 4 to 6

> *1 tablespoon unrefined sesame oil*
> *1 onion, diced*
> *2 stalks celery, chopped*
> *4 cups water*
> *1 cup dried lentils*
> *1/2 teaspoon sea salt*
> *pinch of marjoram*
> *1 bay leaf*
> *1 tablespoon tamari soy sauce*

✄ Heat a soup pot. Add the oil, onion, and celery

and saute. Add the water and bring to a boil.
Wash the lentils and add them to the soup and
simmer 45 minutes. Add the salt, marjoram and
bay leaf and continue cooking 45 minutes or
longer. Add the tamari. Remove the bay leaf
before serving.

SOYBEAN CHILI

1 cup soybeans
1 cup whole grain wheat
6 cups water
1 teaspoon chili powder
1/4 teaspoon red pepper, 1/4 teaspoon oregano
1 clove minced garlic
2 chopped onions
2 chopped jalapeno green chilies
4 chopped tomatoes
2 tablespoons unrefined oil
tamari soysauce

Soak beans and wheat overnight with plenty of
water. Next day pot cook them for 3 or 4 hours.
Add remaining ingredients. Simmer until beans
and wheat are tender. Season with soy sauce or
salt. Garnish with chopped green onions or a
spoonful of guacamole.

SPROUT SOUP
SERVES 4 to 6

4 cups soup stock
2 cups fresh soybean sprouts
2 teaspoons sea salt
2 eggs
tamari to taste
Garnish: scallion greens, sliced on long diagonal

Bring the stock to a boil. Add the sprouts and
salt. Simmer 10 minutes. Remove from heat.

Beat the eggs with a fork and slowly pour into
the soup, stirring constantly. Add tamari to taste
and garnish with scallion greens.

BEAN SPROUT SOUP
SERVES 6

   5 cups water
   3 cups mungbean sprouts
   3 hard boiled eggs, diced
   1/4 cup tamari soy sauce
   6 sprigs parsley

Warm the water. Add sprouts, eggs, tamari, and
parsley. Simmer 5 minutes. Season to taste.

SPROUTED LENTIL SOUP

   2 tablespoons oil
   2 cups sprouted lentils (see sprout chart)
   1 onion, chopped
   1/4 cup soy flour
   1/4 cup whole wheat flour
   6 cups water

Saute lentils and onions for about 5 minutes in
oil. Stir in the flours. Add the water and cook
to taste. Garnish with parsley.

SQUASH STEW
SERVES 6

   2 tablespoons unrefined oil
   1/4 cup sesame seed
   1 onion, chopped
   3 yellow squash, chopped
   1/4 cup whole wheat flour
   2 cups cooked soy flakes
   6 cups water

>⊂ Saute sesame seeds, onions, and squash in the
oil. Stir in flour and flakes. Then add water
and cook until tender. Season to taste as you
simmer until flavor is just right.

TAMARI BOUILLON
YIELD: 4 CUPS

> 1 tablespoon unrefined safflower oil
> 1 small onion, thinly sliced
> 1 clove garlic, finely chopped
> 5 cups water
> 1 tablespoon parsley, chopped
> 1 carrot, thinly sliced
> 2 tablespoons tamari soy sauce

>⊂ Heat a large saucepan. Add the oil, onion, and
garlic and saute. Add the water and all the vegetables. Simmer 30 minutes. Add the soy sauce
and simmer 5 more minutes, and salt to taste.
Leave the vegetables in the broth or strain them
out and use elsewhere. Use as stock for other
soups.

OKRA SOUP
SERVES 6

> 1/2 cup oil
> 2 cups okra, diced
> 2 carrots, diced
> 1 onion, chopped
> 1 cup wheat flakes
> 6 cups water

>⊂ Saute all ingredients in oil. Add water and sim-
mer till tender. Season to taste.

WHOLE GRAIN OR FLAKE SOUP
SERVES 6

> *3 tablespoons unrefined sesame or*
> *safflower oil*
> *1 large onion, thinly sliced*
> *3 stalks celery, finely chopped*
> *2 cups cooked whole grain (rice, buckwheat,*
> *millet) or 1 cup uncooked whole grain*
> *flakes*
> *4 cups tamari broth, vegetable stock or water*
> *1 tablespoon chopped chives*
> *1 tablespoon chopped parsley*
> *1 teaspoon sea salt*
> *sea salt to taste*

Heat a large saucepan. Add the oil, onions, and
celery and saute. Add the cooked grains, or
uncooked grain flakes and saute. Add the broth
and seasonings, cover and simmer 30 minutes, or
until slightly thickened. Season to taste.

WATERCRESS SOUP
SERVES 4

> *2 tablespoons unrefined safflower oil*
> *2 cups chopped green onions*
> *1 large bunch watercress (about 2*
> *cups after trimming off stems)*
> *3 tablespoons whole wheat flour*
> *1 teaspoon crushed basil*
> *2 cups water or vegetable stock*
> *1 cup milk*
> *1 cup yogurt*
> *Garnish chopped watercress or chopped parsley*

Heat a large saucepan. Add the oil, onions and
watercress and saute until just wilted. Stir in the
flour, salt, tamari, and basil. Cook stirring con-

stantly, 1 minute until the mix bubbles. Add the
water or broth. Bring to simmer and cook 10
minutes. Cool. Stir in the milk and yogurt. Serve
hot or cold.

AVOCADO SOUP
SERVES 6

> *2 cups water*
> *2 cups tomato juice*
> *1 carrot, finely chopped*
> *3 stalks celery, finely chopped*
> *1 small onion, finely chopped*
> *2 tomatoes, finely chopped*
> *2 avocados, mashed*

Mix all ingredients well in sauce pan. Add sea
salt or kelp and herbs to taste. Heat, stirring constantly, till just hot.

TOMATO SOUP
SERVES 6

> *3 cups tomato juice*
> *2 tomatoes, finely chopped*
> *1 onion, finely chopped*
> *1 green pepper, finely chopped*
> *1/4 cup almond nut butter*
> *3 tablespoons tamari soy sauce*

Combine all ingredients in a sauce pan. Stir until
nut butter is dissolved. Heat until very warm,
stirring constantly.

VEGETABLE-SOY-SESAME SOUP

SERVES 8

> 1/2 cup unrefined oil
> 1 cup carrots, diced
> 1/2 cup celery, chopped
> 2 onions, chopped
> green pepper, chopped
> tomato, chopped
> 1/2 cup sesame seeds
> 1/2 cup whole wheat flour
> 2 cups cooked soy flakes
> 6 to 8 cups water
> 1/4 cup tamari

>< Saute the vegetables and seeds in the oil. Stir in flour. Add flakes and water, and simmer till tender. Add tamari. Season to taste.

WHOLE GRAIN SOUP

SERVES 6

> 1 cup whole wheat berries or other
>   whole grains
> 6 cups boiling water
> 2 tablespoons soy flour
> 2 onions, chopped
> 2 carrots, chopped
> tamari soy sauce

>< Add wheat berries to water and cook 1 hour until almost tender. Make paste with soy flour and water and add. Add other ingredients and simmer 30 minutes. Add tamari to taste.

VEGETABLES

CHOP SUEY
SERVES 6

> 4 tablespoons unrefined oil
> 1 onion, chopped
> 5 stalks celery, chopped
> 1 cup sliced mushrooms
> 4 cups mungbean sprouts

>< Saute vegetables in the oil, beginning with onions, then celery, mushrooms and sprouts. Add 1/4 cup water and cover. Steam until tender (about 5 minutes). Add tamari and seasonings to taste.

GREEN BEANS AND SUNFLOWER SEEDS
SERVES 4

> 1 pound green beans
> 6 tablespoons butter
> 1/2 cup sunflower seeds
> sea salt to taste

>< Steam green beans until tender. In a large frying pan, melt butter over low heat. Add beans, sunflower seeds, and salt. Increase to medium heat. Stir gently until seeds are lightly browned.

BEET RELISH

> 2 cups beets, cooked, diced
> 2 cups mungbean sprouts
> 1/2 cup chopped onion
> 1 tablespoon raw honey
> 1 teaspoon sea salt
> 1/2 cup apple cider vinegar

>< Mix in large bowl. Stir in vinegar and a squeeze of lemon. Cover and refrigerate for a couple of days.

CARROTS, BROCCOLI AND PUMPKIN SEEDS

SERVES 4

> 3 tablespoons unrefined oil
> 6 carrots, sliced diagonally
> 3 stalks of broccoli, chopped
> 1 large onion, sliced thin
> 1/2 cup pumpkin seeds

>< Heat a skillet on medium heat. Add the oil and cut up vegetables. Saute over low heat until crisply tender. Add the pumpkin seeds and just heat through. Vegetables and seeds should be crunchy-tender.

GREEK GREENS

SERVES 4

> 2 pounds fresh spinach, or other greens
> 1 tablespoon unrefined olive oil
> 1/2 cup pine nuts or sesame seeds
> 1 clove garlic, minced
> 1 small onion, finely chopped
> 2 tablespoons cider vinegar
> sea salt or tamari to taste

>< Wash and tear the greens, removing heavy stems. Heat a large skillet. Add the oil and nuts and saute until golden. Add all the other ingredients. Stir, cover, and cook 2 minutes, until the greens are barely tender.

SESAME GREEN BEANS

> 4 cups green beans or Italian green beans or any crisp vegetable eaten cooked
> 1 tablespoon unrefined sesame oil
> 1 tablespoon sesame seeds
> Sesame salt or sea salt to taste

>< Cook the beans with the minimum amount of water. They should be slightly crisp when done. Drain any excess liquid but save for sauces. Heat

a skillet on medium heat. Add the oil and sesame
seeds and stir until the seeds begin to sizzle. Add
the beans. Stir gently and heat through. Season
to taste.

LIMAS AND VEGETABLES
SERVES 6

>   1 quart boiling water
>   2 cups dry lima beans
>   1/2 teaspoon pepper
>   1 teaspoon sea salt
>   2 tablespoons unrefined oil
>   2 carrots, diced
>   1 onion, chopped
>   2 tablespoons parsley, chopped

Slowly add beans to boiling water. Reduce heat,
cover and simmer 1-1/2 hours or until almost
tender adding more water if necessary. Add
other ingredients and continue cooking until all
is tender, about 45 minutes.

MILLET PUREE
SERVES 4

>   1 tablespoon unrefined oil
>   1 cauliflower, cut up in small pieces
>   1 1/2 cups millet
>   7 cups water
>   1/2 teaspoon sea salt

Heat a large saucepan. Add the oil and cauliflower and saute until golden. Add the millet
and saute until lightly browned. Add the water
and salt and bring to a boil. Reduce heat and
simmer 1 hour. Put the mixture through a food
mill. Serve with gravy.

FRIED OKRA
SERVES 4

> 1 pound okra
> yellow cornmeal
> unrefined oil
> sea salt

Cut okra about 3/8 inch thick, rinse and drain. Shake rounds of okra in a bag with cornmeal and fry till crisp in the oil. Season to taste.

PEAS & CHEESE
SERVES 6

> 3 tablespoons unrefined oil
> 1 onion, finely chopped
> 1 clove garlic, minced
> 1 tablespoon raw honey
> 4 cups cooked split peas, mashed
> 1/2 cup grated cheese

Saute the onion and garlic in the oil. Blend in remaining ingredients except cheese. Cover and heat through. Garnish with the cheese.

BAKED PINTOS
SERVES 8

> 2 cups dry pinto beans
> 5 cups water
> 2 small onions, chopped
> 1 cup stewed tomatos, or tomato sauce
> 1/4 cup molasses
> 1/4 cup tamari soy sauce
> 1 tablespoon chili powder

Add pintos to water. Cover and simmer until tender, 2 to 3 hours. Add other ingredients and simmer till tender and tasty.

RED & GREEN PINTOS
SERVES 6

> 4 cups cooked pintos
> 1 cup cooking water from pintos
> 2 tablespoons unrefined oil
> 2 cloves garlic, minced
> 1 pound fresh spinach, chopped
> 1 hot red pepper, minced
> sea salt to taste
> pinch of cayenne

Saute garlic in the oil. Add the spinach and stir for two or three minutes. Add beans, pepper and seasoning. Stir over high heat until beans are lightly browned. Add cooking water, and simmer a few minutes.

HONEYED SWEET POTATOES
SERVES 6

> 3 large sweet potatoes
> 1/4 cup sunflower seeds
> 2 tablespoons unrefined oil
> 1/4 cup raw honey

Bake sweet potatoes until tender. Cut in half, lengthways, and baste with oil, honey and sunflower seeds. Bake a few more minutes.

DUTCH OVEN POTATOES
SERVES 1 POTATO PER PERSON

> A dutch oven with lid. A pan that fits inside the oven. Optional: foil for wrapping potatoes, butter, sea salt, yogurt

Scrub the potatoes. Puncture the skins. Oil lightly, wrap in foil if desired. Place the potatoes in the pan. If the potatoes are not wrapped, oil the pan and add a little water. Place pebbles in the bottom of the dutch oven. Place the pan of potatoes on the pebbles. Cover and set the dutch oven into hot coals. Place hot coals on the lid too. Bake about an hour. Serve with butter, salt, and yogurt if desired.

PARMESAN POTATOES
SERVES 6

>
> 3 large baking potatoes
> 1/2 cup yogurt
> 1/2 cup grated parmesan cheese
> 2 tablespoons butter
> 1/2 teaspoon sea salt

Oil the skins and bake the potatoes 1 hour at 400 degrees. Cut the potatoes in half lengthwise. Scoop out the shells. Mix the potato with the yogurt, cheese, butter, and salt. Refill the shells. Place the filled shells in an oiled baking dish. Bake 10 to 15 minutes at 400 degrees or until heated through.

POTATOES FOR A MOB
SERVES 18

>
> 18 thin skinned potatoes, cut up
> 1 cup unrefined corn oil
> 1 cup tamari soy sauce

Boil potatoes until tender. Mash coarsely on a large oiled grill. Stir in oil and tamari. Saute a few onion rings and zucchini on the side, and you are half-way home with the meal for the mob.

POTATO PANCAKES
YIELD: 6 CAKES

> 1 onion, diced
> 1/2 teaspoon sea salt
> 2 cups cold, cooked potatoes, mashed
> 2 tablespoons parsley
> whole wheat flour
> optional: 1 egg

>— Mix the onion, salt, the mashed potatoes, and the egg, if desired. Add the parsley and enough flour to hold them together. Fry in oil until brown on one side. Turn and brown on the other side.

SCALLION TAMARI

> 1 bunch scallions, chopped
> 1/2 cup water
> 1/2 cup tamari soy sauce

>— Mix the water and tamari. Cover the scallions with the liquid. Marinate 3 to 4 hours. Serve as a condiment with rice or other grains. This sauce is very tangy.

COOKED MUNGBEAN SPROUTS
SERVES 6

> 3 tablespoons unrefined oil
> one onion, finely chopped
> 2 cups mungbean sprouts
> 2 tablespoons tamari soy sauce

>— Saute chopped onion in the oil. Add sprouts and cook just until heated through. Add tamari. Garnish with herbs.

TOMATO & SPROUTS
SERVES 6

> 3 tablespoons unrefined oil
> one onion, finely chopped
> 1/2 cup celery, chopped
> 1 bell pepper, chopped
> 1 cup mungbean sprouts
> 2 cups stewed tomatoes

Saute onion, celery and pepper in the oil. Add other ingredients. Cover and steam until tender.

BAKED SQUASH
SERVES 6

> 3 squash
> 1/4 cup raw honey
> 3 tablespoons unrefined oil
> 1 tablespoon tamari soy sauce
> 1/4 cup sesame seeds
> 1/4 cup sunflower seeds

Cut squash into two parts, lengthwise. Scoop out seeds. Mix remaining ingredients and fill centers of squash pieces. Place in shallow pan with a little water in the bottom. Cover and bake about an hour at 300 degrees. Remove lid and bake till glazed and done.

YOGURT BROILED TOMATOES
SERVES 4

> 6 to 8 slices of tomato
> 1/2 cup homemade yogurt
> 1/2 cup bread crumbs
> 1 small clove garlic, finely minced
> 1 small onion, finely minced
> 2 tablespoons chopped fresh parsley

Mix all ingredients together. Spread on tomatoes (1 heaping tablespoon per slice). Broil until lightly browned.

ZUCCHINI CAKES

YIELD: 2 dozen cakes

6 medium zucchini, grated and drained
1 onion, minced
1 garlic clove, finely minced
4 eggs, beaten
1 cup whole wheat flour
1 teaspoon sea salt
1/4 cup chopped parsley
pepper to taste
Unrefined oil for frying (safflower or
    peanut oil)

Mix all the ingredients well. Add more flour
if necessary to make a thick batter. Drop by
the tablespoon into a hot, well oiled skillet.
Fry until golden. Turn and brown the other
side.

STOVED POTATOES

— From Laurelbrook Foods, Bel Air, Maryland

New potatoes
Dulse
Sea salt

Pick potatoes of the same size. Scrub and put in
pot with no more than 1 inch of water. Sprinkle
with a little salt (or use sea water and no salt).
Rinse a small amount of dulse, about 1/2 cup
dry for every 5 potatoes. Add to pot. Dot with
butter. Cover tightly and simmer gently till done,
30-45 minutes.

MAIN DISHES

BULGHUR-SOY PILAFF

SERVES 6

3 tablespoons unrefined safflower oil
1/2 cup chopped onions
2 cups bulghur-soy grits or cracked wheat
3 1/2 cups boiling water
sea salt to taste
1/4 cup toasted sunflower seeds

Brown onions in the oil in a saucepan. Remove from heat and stir in grits so that all grains are coated with oil. Add boiling water and salt. Turn mixture into a 2-quart baking dish. Cover and bake 45 minutes at 375 degrees. Garnish with the sunflower seeds.

BURRITOS

1 dozen whole wheat flour tortillas
1 tablespoon unrefined oil
2 small uncooked jalapeno peppers, chopped
3 cups cooked pinto beans, mashed

Heat a skillet. Add the oil and the chopped peppers and saute 5 minutes. Add the beans and cook them until almost dry. Then put 1 to 2 tablespoons of the mixture in a tortilla and roll. For a different taste dip tortilla in hot oil. Then fill with the mixture and roll. Delicious either way.

CORN MUSH
SERVES 8

> 1-1/2 cups stoneground cornmeal
> 1/2 cup soy flour
> 1 teaspoon sea salt
> 1/2 teaspoon sage
> 7 cups cold water

>< Mix meal, flour and sage. Stir in the water and salt slowly. Bring to simmer. Cover and cook about 45 minutes. Include a few chopped jalapeno peppers and tamari if you like.

ITALIAN PIE
SERVES 10

> 1 recipe for corn mush for crust
> 1 pound natural cheese, cubed
> 1/4 cup chopped ripe olives
> 2 or 3 cloves garlic, minced
> 2 onions, chopped
> 1/2 cup chopped, cooked chili peppers
> 1 cup tomato sauce
> 1 tablespoon unrefined oil
> 1 tablespoon oregano
> 1 egg, beaten

>< Spread mush in an oiled, flat 2 quart baking dish. Bake 15 minutes at 425 degrees. Mix all remaining ingredients together. Spread over hot mush crust. Bake at 350 degrees until set and cheese melts. This is a real winner.

CORNMEAL SPOON BREAD
SERVES 6

2 cups cold milk or stock
1 cup stoneground yellow cornmeal
1 cup milk or water
2 eggs, beaten
1 tablespoon unrefined oil
1 teaspoon sea salt

➤ Stir cold liquid into cornmeal in a saucepan. Slowly bring to a boil, stirring constantly. Remove from heat and stir in remaining ingredients. Pour into an oiled square cake pan. Bake 25 to 30 minutes at 400 degrees.

STUFFED EGGS
SERVES 6-8

6 hard boiled eggs, peeled
2 tablespoons mayonnaise
1 teaspoon fresh lemon juice
Sea salt or seasoned sea salt
1/2 teaspoon black pepper
Garnish: Finely chopped parsley
Paprika

➤ Cut eggs in halves. Mash yolks with remaining ingredients. Fill egg whites with yolk mixture. Sprinkle half of the eggs with finely chopped parsley, the other half with paprika.

GNOCCHI
SERVES 4

1 cup plus 1 tablespoon water
pinch sea salt
5 tablespoons butter
1 cup sifted whole wheat pastry flour

6 *eggs*
2 *cups rich cream sauce, thinned with extra milk*
2 *cups grated Swiss cheese*

>< Mix water, sea salt and butter in a pan. Bring to
a boil and add flour all at once. Remove from
fire while stirring with a wooden spoon until it
forms a ball. Beat in two eggs. Beat in the remaining four eggs and mix well. Put a cloth over
the top of the pan and let rest for at least 2
hours. In a large pan put plenty of water and
bring to the simmering point. Work with 2 teaspoons, filling one with the dough and pushing
it out of the spoon with the other into the simmering water. When the dumpling-like balls
come to the top (about 10 minutes), lift them
out and drain. When dry, put in a buttered
casserole. Cover with a thin, cream sauce and
grated cheese. Bake 20 minutes at 350 degrees.

SPROUT BURGERS
YIELD: Twelve 1/2 inch thick patties

2 *cups soy bean sprouts and wheat sprouts*
    mixed
1/2 *cup sunflower seeds*
1/2 *cup sesame seeds*
2 *cups soft cooked whole grain (Brown rice,*
    buckwheat, barley or millet) cooked
    without seasoning.
4 *tablespoons nut butter (peanut or sesame)*
1 *small onion, finely chopped*
1 *to 2 tablespoons tamari soy sauce*
Optional seasoning: Sea salt, sage, thyme
    (up to 1/2 teaspoon each)
1/2 *cup whole wheat flour and/or soft*
    bread crumbs.

➤ Mix all ingredients well. Shape into 1/2 inch thick patties. It may be necessary to add a little more flour or a little water to make the mix hold together. Dust the patties with flour. Fry in a little oil on low to moderate heat until golden outside and heated through. Serve on home-made buns with all the fixings. Mung bean sprouts may be substituted for part of the sprouts for a surprising fresh flavor.

Filling for TORTILLAS

Any cooked grains or beans
chopped onions
chopped peppers
sea salt
chili ·powder
cumin powder
ground red pepper

➤ Mix all ingredients to taste, adding enough cook-ing oil to make a moist mixture. Put a heaping tablespoonful on a tortilla. Add grated cheese. Roll. Place rolled tortillas in a baking pan. Pour seasoned beans and juice over. Bake until heated through. Top with more grated cheese. Top with a little yogurt if you wish.

FRIJOLES
SERVES 6

3 cups cooked and mashed pinto beans
1 clove garlic, minced
1 onion, grated
1 teaspoon sea salt
pinch of oregano
1/2 cup grated.cheese

➤ Mix all ingredients. Cook in top of double boiler over hot water until cheese is melted. Makes a good filling for tortillas too.

BASIC BEANS
SERVES 8

> 5 cups boiling water
> 2 cups dry pinto beans, rinsed

>⊂⊃ Add the beans to the water. Cover tightly and simmer on low heat 2-1/2 to 3 hours or until tender. Beans should not be seasoned until after they are tender. Then add sea salt, chili powder, chopped onions and a little unrefined oil. Simmer a little while longer.

BASIC SOYBEANS
SERVES 8

> 2 cups dry soybeans
> 6 cups water

>⊂⊃ Soak overnight. Next day add more water if needed. Cover and simmer 2 to 3 hours or until tender. Do not season until after the soybeans are tender.

BASIC GRAIN FLAKES
SERVES 8

> 2 cups flaked wheat, oats, rye or rice
> 4 cups boiling water

>⊂⊃ Add flakes to water. Cover and simmer 15 minutes. Season to taste.

BASIC SOY FLAKES

> *1 cup soy flakes*
> *2 cups boiling water*
> *1 teaspoon lime juice*

⤳ Add soy flakes to the water. Reduce heat. Cover and simmer 1-1/2 hours. The skins will rise to the top and will need to be stirred back in. Add lime juice. Flakes are ready to be used in any recipe. Do not salt until done.

BASIC BULGHUR-SOY GRITS, Cracked GRAINS, or BULGHUR

> *2 cups water*
> *1 teaspoon sea salt*
> *1 cup bulghur-soy grits, cracked wheat,*
> *   or bulghur*

⤳ Bring water to a full boil. Add salt and grits. Reduce heat, cover and simmer until grits are tender.

BASIC WHOLE GRAINS

SERVES 8

> *4 cups seasoned stock*
> *2 cups whole grain wheat, rye, rice, bulghur,*
> *   or barley*
> *2 tablespoons unrefined oil*
> *1/4 cup chopped parsley*

⤳ Boil stock in top of double boiler over direct heat. Add remaining ingredients. Cover and set over bottom of double boiler containing hot water. Cook over low heat until all liquid is absorbed. Season to taste.

⤳ Alternate Method: Bring stock to boil. Add grain. Cover and simmer over low heat until liquid is absorbed, 1 to 1-1/2 hours. Add remaining ingredients.

BASIC MILLET

>   *4 cups boiling water*
>   *1 cup millet*

Add millet to water. Cover and simmer 20 to 30 minutes. Season to taste.

BASIC BUCKWHEAT

>   *2 cups buckwheat groats*
>   *hot water to cover*

Pour liquid over buckwheat. Cover and simmer about 15 minutes. Season to taste.

BROCCOLI CASSEROLE

SERVES 8

>   *1/2 cup unrefined oil*
>   *1 cup rye flakes or wheat flakes*
>   *2 onions, chopped*
>   *3 cups chopped broccoli·*
>   *3 cups milk*
>   *1/2 cup soy flour*

Saute flakes, onions and brococli in the oil. Add milk and cook until tender. Stir in soy flour, adding water if necessary. Simmer until liquids form thick sauce. Pour in casserole dish. Top with cheese. Bake until cheese melts.

SPINACH CASSEROLE

SERVES 4

>   *2 cups cooked grain flakes or brown rice*
>   *3/4 cup grated cheddar or goat cheese*
>   *2 eggs, beaten*
>   *2 tablespoons chopped parsley*
>   *1/2 teaspoon sea salt*
>   *1 pound fresh spinach, chopped*
>   *2 tablespoons wheat germ*
>   *2 tablespoons unrefined oil*

⊱Combine the cooked grain flakes and cheese.
Combine the eggs, parsley and salt. Add the two
mixtures and stir into the raw spinach. Pour
into an oiled 1 quart casserole. Top with wheat
germ which has been mixed with the oil. Bake
25 to 35 minutes at 350 degrees.

RICE, WHEAT OR RYE FLAKES CASSEROLE
SERVES 4-6

> *1 tablespoon unrefined oil*
> *2 cups rice, wheat or rye flakes*
> *4 cups water*
> *1/2 teaspoon sea salt*
> *1 tablespoon unrefined oil*
> *1 onion, chopped*
> *3 zucchini, chopped or 2 cups bean sprouts*
> *1/4 pound cheese, grated (1 cup)*

⊱Heat a skillet. Add the oil and flakes and saute
until lightly toasted. Add the water and the salt.
Cover and simmer 20 minutes. Saute the onions
and zucchini in oil for 5 minutes. Add cheese
and vegetables to flakes. Bake 30 minutes at
350 degrees.

TOMATO, SOY & RICE
SERVES 8

> *1/4 cup unrefined oil*
> *1 cup brown rice*
> *1 cup soy flakes*
> *5 cups water*
> *2 tablespoons unrefined oil*
> *1 cup stewed tomatoes*
> *2 onions, chopped*
> *1/4 cup sesame seeds*

><> Saute rice and soy flakes in the oil for 5 minutes. Add water and simmer till tender, about 1-1/2 hours. Saute onions and tomatoes in more oil and stir into grains. Garnish with sesame seeds and season to taste with tamari or sea salt and herbs.

VEGETABLE, FLAKE LAYER DISH
SERVES 4 to 6

> *(Good for any left over cooked grains or*
>   *flakes)*
> *2 cups cooked soy bean flakes-or 2 cups of*
>   *a mixture of any cooked grains, beans*
>   *or flakes*
> *2 cups fresh or fresh frozen corn*
> *2 cups stewed tomatoes*
> *2 cups grated cheese*
> *sea salt*

><> In a deep oiled 1-1/2 quart baking dish, make 1 layer each of beans, corn and tomatoes with some cheese and a sprinkle of salt on each layer. Put the remaining cheese on top. Cover and bake 15 minutes at 350 degrees or until the corn is tender.

GRAIN CASSEROLE
SERVES 6

> *2 cups cooked millet*
> *2 cups cooked rice or other cooked grain*
> *1 egg, beaten*
> *2 tablespoons tamari soy sauce*
> *1/4 cup unrefined oil*
> *2 cups cooked vegetables, chopped fine*
> *1 teaspoon sage*

>< 1 teaspoon oregano
Optional: 1/2 cup chopped nuts
2 cups grated cheese

Mix all the ingredients except the cheese. Place in an oiled 2 quart casserole dish and top with grated cheese. Bake 20 minutes at 400 degrees. This is a good recipe for using leftovers.

TASTY BUCKWHEAT
SERVES 4-6

3 tablespoons unrefined oil
1 large onion, chopped
3 tablespoons whole wheat flour
2 cups water
pinch of sage
4 cups cooked buckwheat

Heat a heavy pan. Add the oil and the onion, and saute until transparent. Stir in the flour until browned. Add the water and stir until slightly thickened. Add sage and the cooked buckwheat. Turn into an oiled 2 quart casserole. Bake 30 minutes at 350 degrees. The sage does it!

MILLET AND WHEAT (like a pilaf)
SERVES 4

6 cups water
1/2 cup whole grain wheat (may be dry, soaked or sprouted)
1 tablespoon unrefined oil
1 cup millet
1 tablespoon unrefined oil
2 bunches scallions, chopped
Tamari soy sauce
sesame tahini

Fill a pot with the water. Add the wheat berries.
Bring to a boil. While the wheat is boiling, heat
a large skillet. Add the oil and millet and saute
until toast brown. Add the boiling mixture to
the millet. Simmer about 20 minutes until the
water is gone. The millet should be fluffy and
the wheat berries chewy. Saute the scallions in
oil in the first pot. Mix them with the cooked
grains. Serve with tamari and tahini.

BULGHUR AND VEGETABLES
SERVES 6

> 1 cup cracked wheat or bulghur, millet,
>   or buckwheat
> 1 1/2 teaspoons sea salt
> 3 cups boiling water
> 4 tablespoons unrefined oil
> 1/2 cup chopped onions
> 1/2 cup chopped green pepper
> 1/2 cup chopped celery
> 6 large tomatoes, chopped
> 1 tablespoon raw honey

Add the grain and salt to the boiling water. Stir,
cover and cook on low heat for 20 minutes. Heat
a large heavy skillet. Add the oil and vegetables
and saute 5 minutes. Add the sauteed vegetables
to the wheat. Add the honey. Cook slowly until
thick.

GREEN RICE
SERVES 6

> 3 cups hot cooked brown rice
> 1 cup chopped parsley
> 1/4 cup tamari soy sauce
> 1/4 cup toasted sesame seeds
> 3 tablespoons unrefined oil

>◦ Mix all ingredients. Serve with additional herbs to taste.

RICE WITH CHEESE
SERVES 4

>   2 cups cooked brown rice
>   3 tablespoons unrefined oil
>   1 onion, chopped
>   1 clove garlic, minced
>   2 cups milk
>   1 cup grated cheese
>   3 tablespoons chopped parsley

>◦ Saute onion and garlic in the oil. Add milk, rice and half the cheese. Mix well. Turn into an oiled casserole dish. Sprinkle remaining cheese on top. Bake 30 minutes at 350 degrees. Garnish with parsley.

CRUNCHY RICE
SERVES 4

>   2 cups cooked rice
>   2 cups grated cheese
>   1/2 teaspoon sea salt
>   2 cups milk
>   3 eggs, beaten
>   one onion, chopped
>   3 tablespoons chopped parsley
>   1 cup slivered almonds
>   1/4 cup sunflower seeds

>◦ Combine all ingredients. Turn into an oiled casserole dish. Bake 35 minutes at 350 degrees.

RICE & ALMOND CASSEROLE
SERVES 8

    4 cups cooked brown rice
    4 eggs, beaten
    4 cups milk
    1/4 cup unrefined oil
    1 tablespoon tamari soy sauce
    1 cup almonds, chopped
    1 cup chopped mushrooms (optional)

Mix all ingredients together. Bake 20 minutes at 350 degrees.

HUEVOS RANCHEROS ON RICE
SERVES 6

    2 cups water
    4 tomatoes, chopped
    1 cup raw rice
    2 tablespoons unrefined oil
    1 onion, chopped
    1 green pepper, chopped
    1 teaspoon sea salt
    1 teaspoon paprika
    6 eggs

Bring the water and tomatoes to a boil. Add the rice. Cover and simmer about 40 minutes. Saute the onions and peppers in oil until soft. Add to the cooked rice. Add salt and paprika. Mix. Make 6 indentations in the rice. Drop one egg in each indentation. Cover and continue to simmer until eggs are set (5 minutes to 10). Serve with chili and tomato sauce if desired.

SCRAMBLED RICE

SERVES 6-8

> 3 tablespoons unrefined oil
> 1 onion, finely chopped
> 4 cups cooked brown rice
> 8 eggs, beaten
> 1 teaspoon sea salt or 1 tablespoon tamari soy
>   sauce
> chopped chives, pepper to taste
> Optional: left over chopped vegetables

Heat a large, heavy skillet. Add the oil, onion, and rice and saute 5 minutes. Add the eggs and the salt and cook on low heat stirring frequently until eggs are set. Add chives, pepper or other seasonings as desired. Add left-over vegetables and heat through.

BULGHUR-SOY VEGETABLE LOAF

SERVES 6

> 2 cups cooked bulghur-soy grits, cracked
>   wheat, or grain flakes
> 3 carrots, grated
> 1 onion, finely chopped
> 1 cup stewed tomatoes
> 2 eggs, beaten
> 1/4 cup soy flour
> 1/4 cup wheat germ
> 1/4 tamari soy sauce

Mix all ingredients. Bake in oiled loaf pan at 350 degrees for about an hour.

RYE LOAF
SERVES 8

1 cup cooked whole grain rye or other
      cooked whole grain
2 cups cooked beans
3 cups bread crumbs moistened in 1 cup water
2 chopped onions
1 grated carrot
3 tablespoons parsley
1 teaspoon salt
1 tablespoon tamari soy sauce
1 tablespoon unrefined oil

Mix all ingredients in a bowl. Pour into an oiled loaf pan. Bake 45 minutes at 375 degrees.

LENTIL SOY LOAF
SERVES 6

1 cup cooked lentils
1 cup cooked soybeans or soybean flakes
2 cups whole wheat bread crumbs
1/4 cup chopped parsley
2 cups milk
1 teaspoon poultry seasoning

Mix all ingredients. Turn into an oiled loaf pan. Bake 30 to 40 minutes at 350 degrees. Serve with tomato sauce.

LENTIL & TOMATO LOAF
SERVES 6

2 cups cooked lentils
2 tablespoons unrefined oil
1 onion, chopped
3 stalks celery, chopped
3 cups stewed tomatoes
1/4 cup wheat germ
sea salt to taste

⤜Saute onion and celery in the oil. Stir into
lentils. Add stewed tomatoes and simmer. Mix
in wheat germ and salt. Stir in a little whole
wheat flour if needed to thicken. Bake in oiled
loaf pan 30 minutes at 350 degrees.

MILLET LOAF

1-9 x 5" LOAF

> *3 cups cooked millet*
> *5 scallions, chopped*
> *2 carrots, grated*
> *1/2 cup slivered green beans*
> *1/4 to 1/2 cup whole wheat flour*
> *1 cup grated cheese*
> *2 eggs*
> *Garnish: toasted sesame seeds*

⤜Mix all ingredients together and press into an
oiled loaf pan. Bake 1 hour at 350 degrees
Garnish with toasted sesame seeds. The mixture
also makes delicious croquettes.

SOY & MUSHROOM LOAF

SERVES 6

> *2 cups cooked soy flakes*
> *2 teaspoons sea salt*
> *1 cup sliced mushrooms*
> *1 onion, finely chopped*
> *2 tablespoons unrefined oil*
> *2 eggs, beaten*
> *1/2 cup whole wheat flour*
> *1/4 cup sesame seeds*

⤜Mix all ingredients with enough water to make
into loaf consistency. Bake in oiled loaf pan 20
to 30 minutes at 350 degrees.

MILLET PATTIES
YIELD: 8 PATTIES

   3 cups cooked, hulled millet
   1/2 cup sesame butter
   1/2 cup soy flour
   1/4 cup unrefined oil
   tamari soy sauce or sea salt to taste

>< Heat millet. Add soy flour and sesame butter, adding a little water if necessary. Stir in oil and season to taste. Shape into patties. Bake on oiled sheet at 350 degrees till brown. Garnish with toasted sesame seeds.

RICE PATTIES
SERVES 4

   2 cups cooked brown rice
   1/4 cup unrefined oil
   1 egg
   1 teaspoon sea salt
   1/4 cup soy flour
   1/4 cup whole wheat flour

>< Mix all ingredients into soft dough. Shape into patties. Fry in hot oil. Add tamari to taste.

LEFT-OVER RICE

>< Form rice into balls, 2" in diameter, and deep fry in hot unrefined safflower oil until golden and crisp. Add flour to hold the rice together, but this is not necessary if the rice is moist enough. Diced vegetables can also be mixed in if the flour is added. Serve with tamari.

SOY PATTIES
SERVES 6

>   *2 cups cooked soy flakes*
>   *4 tablespoons unrefined oil*
>   *1 cup wheat germ*
>   *1/2 cup triticale or other flour*
>   *2 eggs, beaten*
>   *2 tablespoons tamari soy sauce*

Mix all ingredients adding flour or water to make patties stick together. Shape and fry in hot oil.

STUFFED PEPPERS
SERVES 6

>   *6 bell peppers*
>   *2 cups cooked soy flakes or cooked grain flakes*
>   *1/4 cup chopped onion*
>   *1/4 cup chopped celery*
>   *1/4 cup tomato sauce*
>   *1/4 cup unrefined oil*
>   *1/2 cup wheat germ*

Scoop out inside of peppers. Mix remaining ingredients. Season to taste with sea salt and pepper. Stuff the peppers. Bake 30 minutes at 350 degrees on a rack above water.

STUFFED PEPPERS, SPANISH STYLE
SERVES 4

>   *4 bell peppers, seeded*
>   *2 tablespoons unrefined oil*
>   *1 large onion, chopped*
>   *2 cups cooked brown rice*
>   *1 cup grated cheese*
>   *1 teaspoon sea salt*

2 teaspoons chili powder
1 teaspoon crushed oregano
2 eggs, beaten
Optional: chopped green chilies

✠Heat a large skillet. Add the oil and onion and
saute 5 minutes. Add the rice and heat through.
Stir in all the other ingredients. Remove from
the heat. Steam 4 bell peppers over boiling
water 10 minutes. Stuff the peppers with the
rice mixture. Bake 10 to 15 minutes or until
heated through at 350 degrees.

NOODLES WITH PARSLEY SAUCE
SERVES 4

1 tablespoon unrefined oil
2 onions, sliced
1/4 cup chopped parsley
1/4 cup water
3 tablespoons tamari soy sauce
8 ounces whole wheat noodles, cooked

✠Heat a 1 quart saucepan. Add the oil and saute
the onions and parsley. Add the water and the
tamari and simmer for 10 minutes. Add 1 package cooked noodles and simmer all the ingredients together until heated through.

SPAGHETTI & MUSHROOMS
SERVES 8

2 quarts boiling water
1 pound thin whole wheat spaghetti
2 tablespoons unrefined sesame oil
2 cups sliced mushrooms
2 onions, chopped

➤ Add spaghetti to water and cook 10 minutes. Drain excess water and save for soups. Saute onions and mushrooms in the oil and mix into spaghetti. Add tamari to taste. Garnish with grated cheese.

ZUCCHINI DELIGHT
SERVES 6

> 1/4 cup unrefined oil
> 2 cups chopped zucchini
> 1 onion, chopped
> 2 eggs, beaten
> 1/4 cup wheat germ
> 1/4 cup soy flour

➤ Saute zucchini and onion. Add eggs, wheat germ, and soy flour. Cook over low heat until eggs are set. Season to taste with tamari and herbs.

ZUCCHINI EGG CASSEROLE
SERVES 6

> 2 tablespoons butter
> 1 medium onion, thinly sliced
> 1 pound zucchini, 1/2 inch slices
> 2 teaspoons sea salt
> 1 cup milk
> 6 eggs
> 1 tablespoon tamari soy sauce
> sliced Mozzarella cheese

➤ Melt butter in skillet. Add onion and saute about 10 minutes. Add zucchini and sea salt to onions and saute about 6 minutes. Beat eggs slightly. Add milk and tamari. Pour over vegetable mixture. Place in oiled 1-1/2 quart casserole. Bake about 15 minutes at 350 degrees. Top with Mozzarella cheese slices. Bake about 5 minutes or until cheese melts.

CHEESE SAUCE

> 1 cup fresh milk
> 1-1/2 cups diced natural cheese
> 2 tablespoons stone-ground whole wheat flour
> 1 tablespoon tamari soy sauce or 1 teaspoon
>   sea salt

Heat the milk on low heat until very warm. Add
the cheese dusted with flour. Add tamari and
cook on low heat, stirring occasionally until
thick.

CREAM SAUCE

> 2 tablespoons butter
> 2 tablespoons whole wheat flour
> 1 cup milk
> salt and pepper to taste

Melt butter over low heat. Stir in flour. Slowly
add milk, stirring constantly. Cook on low heat
until thick as desired. Season to taste.

SQUASH MEDLEY — Beth Davis

SERVES 8

> 8 squash (use small succhini and yellow)
> 1 large red or green pepper, chopped.
> 3 large ripe tomatoes, chopped
> 2 medium onions, chopped
> 1/2 lb. cheese, grated
> 1 teaspoon sea salt
> 1/4 teaspoon pepper

Parboil cut up squash for 3 to 5 minutes. Drain
and spread in flat dish. Mix remaining ingredients. Cover squash with mixture. Top
with fine bread crumbs and dot with butter.
Bake 20 minutes at 400 degrees.

The following four recipes are courtesy of Cathy and Tom Swan and the other good folks at Food For Life, Chicago, Ill. (See Source List).

BARLEY RICE BURGERS
SERVES 10 PEOPLE

>   3 cups brown rice
>   2 cups barley
>   1 cup yellow corn meal
>   1/2 cup whole wheat flour
>   1 onion, diced
>   1 clove of garlic
>   a pinch of oregano

Pressure cook the rice and barley in 6-1/2 cups of water for one hour. Let it cool and then mix with the remaining ingredients in a large bowl. Add water until the mixture forms a tight ball in your hand (or if desired, the mixture can be made more moist for a lighter effect). Form into circular flat patties and pan fry until golden crisp.

COOKED CEREAL WITH VEGETABLES
SERVES 2-4 PEOPLE

>   1 cup either rolled oats, cracked wheat,
>   bulghur, or any other cereal
>   3 cups water
>   1/4 teaspoon salt
>   1 teaspoon unrefined sesame or corn oil
>   1 cup of 2 or 3 different vegetables like:
>   Zucchini, carrots, and onions; broccoli,
>   onion, and summer squash; etc.

Put 3 cups of water on to boil. In a 2 quart casserole skillet, heat oil and add sliced vegetables, sauteing for 5 minutes. Add cereal, salt and

boiling water; stir, cover tightly, and let simmer
for 1/2 hour or until cereal is done and vegetables are soft. Add tamari to taste a few minutes
before end of cooking time. Good for children,
traveling, when you're in a hurry, and for
breakfasts.

DULSE AND VEGETABLES
SERVES 4-6 PEOPLE

> *1 package Dulse (2 oz.)*
> *3 carrots*
> *2 zucchini*
> *1 onion*
> *1 tablespoon either Safflower, corn, or*
> *sesame oil (unrefined)*

Rinse and separate the dulse in cold water. Place
in a bowl of water and allow to soak while cut-
ting the vegetables. Saute the onions in oil for
five minutes; add the carrots and continue sauteing for another five minutes; add the zucchini
and season with tamari, and cook for five more
minutes. Drain the dulse and add to the vegetables. Lower the flame and simmer for ten minutes or until the vegetables are soft.

CHICKPEA DIP
SERVES 10-15 PEOPLE

> *4 cups chickpeas*
> *10 cups water*
> *1 teaspoon salt*
> *1 cup sesame tahini*
> *1 cup chopped fresh green onions*
> *3 cloves fresh garlic, or 1/2 teaspoon*
> *powdered garlic*

Soak chickpeas overnight in water that covers them 2 to 3 inches (they will absorb quite a bit). To prepare: In a 6 quart pressure cooker, cook the chickpeas and water for 3 hours. Begin on a high flame and let jiggle for 1 hour, then medium low flame for balance of 3 hours. When cooled down a bit, either mash chickpeas to paste in suribachi with pestle, or put through a food mill adding left over liquid to the mash. Add salt, tahini, garlic and onions, mixing thoroughly. Salt does vary according to taste. Great on crackers, rice cakes, bread, etc.

BAKED RICE — Stephanie Blythe

1 finely chopped onion
1 Tbsp. unrefined sesame oil
2 cups brown rice
3 Tbsp. chopped parsley
1 finely chopped garlic clove
2 Tbsp. sesame seeds

Saute onion in oil. Add the washed rice, parsley and garlic. Continue sauteing, and after five minutes add the sesame seeds. Brown until grains pop softly. Place in covered casserole with 3 cups boiling water, and bake at 350 degrees for 1-1/2 hours.

BREADS

APPLE MUFFINS

1 cup raw honey
1 cup unrefined oil
4 eggs
2-1/2 cups whole wheat flour
2 teaspoons low sodium baking powder
1/2 teaspoon sea salt
1 teaspoon each allspice, nutmeg and cinnamon
1/2 cup non-instant dry milk powder
2 large apples, grated, or
    2 carrots, grated
1 teaspoon vanilla
1 cup chopped nuts

Beat the honey, oil and eggs. Mix all dry ingredients. Add to honey mixture. Stir well. Add and fold together the apple, vanilla and nuts. Bake at 400 degrees for 12 to 15 minutes. Remove from tins and cool.

BANANA OR APPLESAUCE BREAD

3 ripe bananas, mashed (or 1 cup applesauce)
2 eggs, well beaten
1/3 cup raw honey
2 cups whole wheat flour
1 teaspoon sea salt
2 teaspoons low sodium baking powder
1/2 cup chopped nuts

Mix bananas, eggs and honey. Combine dry ingredients and add. If using applesauce, add 1 teaspoon each of allspice, cinnamon and nutmeg with the dry ingredients. Bake in oiled loaf pan 1 hour at 350 degrees.

HARDTACK BISCUITS
SERVES 6

> 1-1/2 cups whole wheat flour
> 1/4 cup soy flour
> 1 cup rice flour
> 1/4 cup sesame seeds
> 2 teaspoons sea salt
> 1-1/4 cups water

Mix dry ingredients well. Add water to make soft dough. Knead well and cut into biscuits. Bake for 30 to 40 minutes at 350 degrees.

WHOLE WHEAT BISCUITS
SERVES 6

> 2 cups whole wheat pastry flour
> 1/4 cup soy flour
> 3 teaspoons low sodium baking powder
> 1/3 cup unrefined oil
> 1 cup milk
> 1 egg, beaten

Mix dry ingredients. Stir in blended liquid ingredients. Add flour or water as needed to make soft dough. Knead 10 to 12 times. Roll out 1/2 inch thick. Cut and place on oiled cookie sheet. Bake 15 to 20 minutes at 450 degrees.

YEAST BISCUITS
YIELD: 12 Biscuits

> 2 cups whole wheat flour
> 1 cup rice flour
> 1/4 cup unrefined oil
> 3/4 teaspoon sea salt
> 1/4 cup roasted sesame seeds
> 1 tablespoon dry yeast
> 1-1/2 cups warm water

Mix the flours, salt, oil and sesame seeds. Dissolve the yeast in warm water and let sit five minutes. Add to the flour. Knead well and let sit

for one hour. Knead again and form into biscuits.
Place on oiled cookie sheet. Cover with damp
cloth and let sit 20 minutes. Bake 30 minutes at
350 degrees.

WHEAT RUSKS

MAKES 3 to 4 DOZEN

2 cups whole wheat flour
2 cups fresh wheat germ
1-1/4 cups milk
1/2 cup unrefined safflower oil
1 tablespoon raw honey
1 teaspoon sea salt
Caraway seeds
Sesame seeds

Mix and knead all the ingredients together except the seeds. Roll the dough 1/4 inch thick.
Cut into sticks about five inches long. Place on
an oiled cookie sheet. Sprinkle some of the
sticks with caraway and others with sesame seeds.
Bake until golden brown at 350 degrees. Dough
may be cut in squares and made into crackers
instead.

DIXIE CORNBREAD

3 cups stoneground cornmeal
1 teaspoon sea salt
3 tablespoons unrefined corn germ oil
2 cups boiling water
1 cup milk
1 egg, beaten
3 teaspoons low sodium baking powder

Mix the cornmeal, salt and oil together. Pour
boiling water over the cornmeal mixture and stir
until well mixed. Add the milk to the mixture
and set aside to cool (about 40 minutes). When

cool, stir in the egg and baking powder. Pour into a hot, well-oiled 8 x 8 inch pan or muffin tins.
Bake 30 to 40 minutes at 425 degrees.

CORN MEAL DUMPLINGS

2 cups cornmeal
1 teaspoon sea salt
1 egg, beaten
boiling water
1/4 cup rice flour

Mix cornmeal and salt. Stir in egg. Pour enough
water over mixture to make a thick paste. Stir
thoroughly and form into small balls. Roll in
rice flour. Drop dumplings into simmering soup
or stew. Cover and continue to cook for 10 to
15 minutes.

MEXICAN CORNBREAD
SERVES 6

1 cup whole wheat flour
1 cup stone ground corn meal
3 rounded teaspoons of low sodium baking
*   powder*
1/2 teaspoon sea salt
1 teaspoon chili powder
2 eggs, beaten
1/2 cup milk
1/2 cup unrefined corn germ oil
1/4 cup finely chopped onion
1/4 cup finely chopped green bell pepper
2 jalapeno peppers, finely chopped

Stir the flour, meal, baking powder, salt and
chili powder together in a large bowl. Add the
eggs, milk, oil, onion and peppers. Beat all
ingredients together about 1 minute. Pour into
an oiled 8 x 8 pan. Bake about 20 minutes at
425 degrees.

BASIC MUFFINS

10 MUFFINS

>   *1 cup mixed whole grain flours*
>   *1/2 teaspoon sea salt*
>   *1 heaping teaspoon low sodium baking powder*
>   *1 tablespoon unrefined oil*
>   *1 egg, beaten*
>   *1 tablespoon dark molasses*
>   *1 cup buttermilk*

Mix dry ingredients. Stir in the oil and rub in well with fingers. Add egg, molasses and buttermilk. Stir well. Fill greased muffin tins a little over half full. Bake 15 to 17 minutes at 450 degrees. These muffins are excellent with 1/2 cup blueberries or other small berries stirred in the batter. Wheat germ may be used as part of the flour.

YEAST BREAD

>   *2½ cups warm water*
>   *2 tablespoons dry yeast*
>   *3 tablespoons unrefined oil*
>   *3 tablespoons raw honey*
>   *6 cups (approx.) whole wheat flour*
>   *2 teaspoons sea salt*

Dissolve yeast in the warm water. Add oil and honey. Mix flour and salt and add. Mix well, working in last of flour with hands. Add more flour if needed. Cover and let rise till double. Shape into 2 loaves kneading a few minutes. Place in oiled loaf pans. Allow to rise again until doubled. Bake 10 minutes at 400 degrees. Reduce heat to 350 degrees and bake 20 minutes more. Turn out on rack to cool.

BREAD VARIATIONS:

1. Triticale Bread: Substitute triticale flour for 1/2 the flour.
2. Substitute any other flour or meal for part of the flour.
3. Add some leftover cooked grain or cereal to the dough for a loaf that will stay moist.
4. Add some fresh sprouts to the dough to speed up rising time and for a different taste.
5. Use different kinds of sweeteners.
6. Use warm milk or stock in place of water.

ELMER'S CORN-PONE
2 LOAVES

2 cups milk
1 cup water
3 tablespoons molasses
2 tablespoons dry yeast
2 teaspoons sea salt
1 cup yellow cornmeal
6 cups whole wheat flour

Mix the liquids together in a saucepan and heat until lukewarm. Add the yeast, salt, and the flours. Mix and let sit for 10 minutes. Knead the dough in 1 more cup of flour for 5 minutes. Place in an oiled bowl. Cover and let rise until double in size. Knead again and shape into 2 loaves. Bake at 350 degrees for 45 minutes. Turn out on rack to cool, and brush the crusts with oil. Cover with towel while cooling.

RICE FLOUR BREAD
2 LOAVES

6 cups brown rice flour
2 teaspoons sea salt
3 cups warm water
2 tablespoons yeast
2 tablespoons raw honey
4 tablespoons unrefined oil

Mix dry ingredients. Dissolve yeast in the water. Add the oil and dry ingredients. Mix well adding more water if needed to make a soft dough. Fill oiled bread pans 3/4 full. Let sit 45 minutes. Bake 30 minutes at 350 degrees or until crust browns and cracks on top.

PLAIN RYE BREAD
1 9 x 5 LOAF

2 cups warm water
1 package dry yeast
2 teaspoons sea salt
1 tablespoon unrefined safflower oil
4 1/2 cups stone ground rye flour

Dissolve the yeast in the water. Add the salt and oil. Stir well. Add the flour and stir for several minutes. Cover the dough and let it rise 2 hours. Knead the dough in more rye flour for 10 minutes. Shape into a loaf. Place the dough in an oiled 9 x 5 inch loaf pan. Allow to rise 30 minutes to 1 hour. Bake 1-1/2 hours at 300 degrees This is a good bread for those allergic to other grains.

FAST WHOLE WHEAT YEAST BREAD

One 9" x 5" loaf

> *13 ounces lukewarm water*
> *1 tablespoon dry yeast*
> *1 teaspoon raw honey*
> *Optional: 2 tablespoons unrefined corn germ*
> *   oil or safflower oil*
> *4 cups whole wheat flour*
> *1 teaspoon sea salt*

Mix the honey in the warm water. Sprinkle the yeast on top of the water. Set aside until frothy, about five minutes. Add the oil if desired to the yeast. Mix the flour and salt. Pour the yeast mixture into the center of the flour. Mix thorcughly, by hand if necessary. Shape the dough into a loaf. Place in an oiled loaf pan. Let rise slightly over the top of the pan, 20 to 30 minutes. Bake 30 to 40 minutes at 350 degrees.

The oil in this recipe is strictly optional. The loaf is delicious either way. It can be made from start to finish in one hour, including baking. Actual mixing time is only 5 to 10 minutes.

QUICK BATTER ROLLS

1 DOZEN

> *1½ cups warm water*
> *2 tablespoons active dry yeast*
> *1/4 cup unrefined corn germ oil*
> *3 tablespoons unsulphured molasses or honey*
> *1 teaspoon sea salt*
> *1 egg, beaten*
> *3 cups whole wheat flour*

Dissolve the yeast in the water. Add oil, molasses, salt, and egg. Mix thoroughly. Add flour and beat until well blended. Cover the dough. Let rise in a warm place until double in bulk, 20 to 30 minutes. Punch down and shape into din-

ner rolls. Place on oiled baking pan. Bake 20
to 30 minutes.

CHEWY BATTER BREAD

SERVES 4

> 1 egg
> 1 teaspoon sea salt
> 1/2 cup cooked brown rice
> 1/2 cup white cornmeal
> boiling water

Beat the egg until light. Add the salt, rice and
cornmeal. Mix well. Stir in boiling water until
mixture becomes as thick as heavy cream. Pour
into an oiled 8 x 8 inch layer cake pan. Bake 20
to 30 minutes at 350 degrees. This recipe makes
a crisp, chewy bread that is good with soup. It is
a good way to use leftover rice.

RAISIN SCONES

SERVES 6

> 1 cup whole wheat flour
> 1/4 cup raisins
> 1/2 teaspoon sea salt
> 3 tablespoons butter, softened
> Sour milk to mix

Combine the flour, raisins and salt in a bowl.
Rub in soft butter until thoroughly mixed.
Pour in the sour milk to make a soft dough. Pat
out in an 8 inch round cake pan and slice like a
pie. Bake for 20 to 25 minutes at 325 degrees.

UNLEAVENED BREAD
1 LOAF

> 1 2/3 cups warm water
> 4 cups whole wheat flour

Pour water in a large bowl. Add 3 cups of flour. Stir. Add the last cup of flour gradually, stirring until the batter is too stiff to stir. Knead in remaining amount of flour. Knead about 20 times, until the water and flour are well mixed. Shape into loaf as you knead. Oil a small loaf pan. Place the loaf in the pan. Cover with a damp towel and let rise in a warm place for 24 hours. In the summer rising time is less, depending on the temperature. The towel should be kept damp throughout the rising time. Bake 1 hour at 350 degrees. The crust will be chewy and hard. If the bread did not rise to the top of the loan pan, bake 30 minutes at 250 degrees and then 350 degrees until crust is hard. Cool on rack.

FLOUR TORTILLAS
2 DOZEN

> 4 cups whole wheat pastry flour
> 1 teaspoon sea salt
> 1/3 cup unrefined oil
> 1 cup warm water

Mix flour and salt. Add oil and work, mixing together with your fingertips. Stir in enough water to make a firm ball of dough. Knead until smooth. Let sit 20 minutes. Pinch off a piece of dough the size of a golf ball. Roll it out on a floured board to a more or less round shape about 4 inches in diameter. Cook on an unoiled

hot griddle or in a skillet, about 2 minutes on
each side. You can salt the griddle to keep the
tortilla from sticking, but it is not really
necessary.

GREEN BUTTER
YIELD: 3/4 CUP

> *1/2 cup butter, softened*
> *2 tablespoons minced parsley*
> *2 tablespoons minced chives*
> *2 tablespoons lemon juice*

>✕◯ Mix all ingredients well. This is especially good
on herb breads.

ALFALFA BUTTER SPREAD
YIELD: 1 CUP

> *1 cup butter, softened*
> *1/3 cup fresh alfalfa sprouts*
> *juice of 1 lemon*
> *1/4 teaspoon sea salt*
> *dash of cayenne pepper*
> *Optional: chopped fresh parsley*

>✕◯ Mix all ingredients together thoroughly.

ALFALFA SPROUT SPREAD
4 SERVINGS

> *1 cup fresh alfalfa sprouts*
> *juice of small lemon*
> *2 tablespoons tahini*
> *1 tablespoons unrefined sesame oil*

>✕◯ Stir sprouts into blend of other ingredients. Sea-
son to taste with sea salt or tamari. Serve on rye
bread or any other good whole grain bread.

CHEESE DIP

YIELD: 3 to 4 CUPS

> 1 tablespoon unrefined safflower oil
> 1 large or 2 medium onions, chopped
> 1/2 cup chopped peppers
> 1-1/2 cups tomato sauce
> 1 pound sharp cheddar cheese, cubed

Heat a saucepan. Add the oil, onions, peppers, and saute. Add the sauce and simmer about 10 minutes until well done and thick. Add the cheese and melt. Serve with toasted tortillas. This dip is good as a sauce on scrambled eggs, too.

PIMIENTO CHEESE SPREAD

2 CUPS

> 1½ cups shredded cheese
> 1 small jar chopped pimiento
> 2 teaspoons juice from pimiento
> 1 tablespoon tamari soy sauce
> 1/2 cup mayonnaise

Mix all ingredients well. They will mix more easily if they are all at room temperature. Let sit until the flavors blend.

CHICKPEA SPREAD

4 SERVINGS

> 1 cup cooked chickpeas
> 1 cup sesame tahini
> 2 tablespoons unrefined olive oil
> juice of 2 lemons
> 2 garlic cloves, finely minced
> sea salt to taste
> chopped parsley

Mash chickpeas well. Combine remaining ingredients and mix well. Spread on bread or crackers.

DRIED FRUIT PRESERVES
1 to 2 CUPS

> *8 ounces dried fruits*
> *2 tablespoons lemon juice*
> *raw honey*

Chop the dried fruits finely. Add the lemon juice and stir. Cover fruit with raw honey. Cover the bowl and let the fruit sit for about 4 to 5 days, until very soft.

BUSTY PEANUT SPREAD

> *1/2 cup soy flour*
> *1/2 cup peanut butter*
> *1/2 cup sesame butter*

Mix all ingredients together. Add water if needed to make spreadable. May be seasoned with herbs if desired.

PEANUT-SESAME SPREAD

> *1 cup old-fashioned peanut butter*
> *1 cup sesame butter*
> *1/2 cup raw honey*
> *1/2 cup sunflower seeds*

Mix well and refrigerate. This is a delicious spread for children.

SOYFLAKE & TAHINI SPREAD

> *2 cups cooked soy flakes*
> *garlic clove, grated*
> *juice of one lemon*
> *2 tablespoons tahini*
> *2 tablespoons tamari soy sauce*

Mash all ingredients into a paste. Add finely chopped raw vegetables as desired.

CHAPATTI — Submitted by Ratana Stephens

2 cups whole wheat flour
1 cup water (scant)

Slowly add water to flour to make a soft dough. Knead until dough is earlobe consistency and no longer sticky. Form into balls size of golfballs. Dip into dry flour and roll out to a 7 inch round (1/4 to 1/8 inch thick). Bake on a dry, preheated heavy iron skillet. When one side changes color, turn over, then press with a cloth using a rotating action. Watch it puff like a football! Spread with butter to keep soft. Delicious with curries or with anything. It takes practice to make perfect chapattis, so we caution practice. Chapattis are the unleavened, wholesome, bread staple of the robust Panjabis and Hunzas. They are now becoming famous in the west as a delicious variety of bread used in many ways. PURIS can be made exactly like chapattis except that after the chapatti has been rolled out, it is then dropped into hot vegetable oil. Remove the puri after it has been fried a golden brown. Delicious! For PARONTA, use the same dough, but larger individual balls about 2-1/2 inches in diameter. Grate raw medium-sized cauliflower or raw potato finely, with finely chopped onion (1/2 onion). Add salt and chili pepper to taste. Add ginger or garam masala to taste (optional). With thumbs, mold a depression into the dough ball and fill with cauliflower or potato mixture (about one heaping tablespoon). Seal and saute in butter or sesame oil on both sides until browned and ready. Serve with butter along with a dish of yogurt or buttermilk. Very solid and filling food—excellent for strenuous activity.

Ratana and Arran Stephens are with Lifestream Natural Foods, Vancouver, B. C. (see Source List). It is always a joy to be their guest. Warm hospitality seems to be the norm among the people who have helped bring back whole grain cooking in North America.

The following four quick bread recipes are from Rod and Margy Coates at Laurelbrook Foods in Maryland.

DROP SCONES

> 2 cups whole wheat pastry flour
> 3/4 teaspoon baking powder
> 1/4 teaspoon salt
> 1 tablespoon honey
> 1/2 cup milk, buttermilk or whey
> 1 egg, beaten

Mix flour, baking powder and salt. Add remaining ingredients, and beat well. Add more liquid if necessary so it is the consistency of thick cream. Heat griddle and grease lightly. Drop by tablespoonfuls, seeing that they do not overlap and are even. Cook on medium heat until little bubbles appear, and bottom is golden brown. Then cook the other side. Serve warm. Makes about 12.

BANNOCKS OR OAT CAKES

> 2/3 cup coarse ground oat flour
> Pinch of soda
> Pinch of salt
> 2 teaspoon oil
> About 1/2 cup hot water

Mix oat flour, salt and soda. Make a well in the center and pour in oil. Stir and add enough water to make a thick paste. Knead well using oat flour to prevent sticking. Roll into 1/4 inch thickness, cut into large circles, sprinkle with a little oat flour and cut in quarters. Cook on medium hot griddle until edges curl slightly. Or bake in 325 degree oven about 20 minutes.

TEA PANCAKES OR CRUMPETS

>   *2 eggs*
>   *2 tablespoons honey*
>   *2 cups whole wheat flour*
>   *1/2 teaspoon salt*
>   *2 tablespoons oil or butter*
>   *1-1/2 cups milk or buttermilk*

Beat eggs well. Add honey. Mix dry ingredients and add alternately with the oil. Slowly add enough milk so batter is consistency of thin cream Oil hot griddle, beat batter well and drop in by large tablespoonsful. spreading it as thinly and evenly as possible. When golden brown. turn and cook other side.

Set them on a clean towel and spread them with butter. jam or honey, and roll up Serve warm.

SHORTBREAD

>   *5 cups pastry flour, whole wheat flour, or*
>   *4 cups pastry and 1 cup rice flour. or*
>   *5 cups fine oat flour*
>   *1 cup butter*
>   *1/3 cup honey*
>   *1/4 teaspoon salt*

Cream butter and honey together till smooth. Add flours and salt. Work in very lightly until mixture resembles pastry dough. Do not knead or roll. but press with hands into one or two rounds. Pinch edges with fingers and prick all over with fork. Bake in 275 degree oven for about 1 hour. Cool before turning out.

CORN BREAD — Stephanie Blythe

> 2 eggs, separated
> 1-1/2 cups water or other liquid
> 1/4 cup unrefined oil
> 1 cup corn meal
> 1 cup pastry or whole/wheat flour
> 2 tsp. low sodium baking powder
> Dash of sea salt

Beat egg yolks. Add liquid, oil and then dry ingredients, which had been mixed together. Beat egg white, and fold in. Bake at 400-degrees for 25 minutes in preheated and oiled cast iron pan.

The following information and recipes are courtesy of my friend Burton Fox, who with the other good folks of Bullfrog Films, Inc., Winnie, Amanda and John, has produced an outstanding film on bread-making called "Earthbread." This film reviews more than 3,000 years of bread history and provides a step-by-step kitchen demonstration on how to make healthful, delicious whole wheat bread. For information on obtaining this film for a showing to a club, a school, or just a group of friends, write Bullfrog Films, Inc., Box 114, Milford Square, Penna. 18935.

BREAD

The making of bread stretches back to when man began to live in caves thousands of years ago. Bread throughout time has been a fundamental source of sustenance. It was also a product into which adulterous ingredients could be easily concealed. The profound economic and religious importance of bread created great pressures on millers and bakers in their production of consistent loaves of bread. Technological innovations in the mid-19th century facilitated the rate of bread production but the loss of valuable nutrients, inherent in the grain, was the price of the faster milling process. Enrichment, an attempt to replace the vitamins and minerals lost in the rapid milling of the grain, is only partially successful. Many of the nutrients are depleted in the grinding and never replaced.

Making bread in the classroom or in the home with whole grains, is one of the few things that can be done, in this age of technology, with a minimum number of ingredients and materials, yet which can produce results that belie, to the nose and the mouth, the simplicity of the process. We share with our primitive brothers a common source of knowledge when we arrange the few basic materials necessary to make bread. In the eating of this food we can make rare connections by saying that way back when, people throughout the world had a similar gastronomical experience.

Bread Is Simple Stuff

To make a simple analogy, bread can be a whistle or an orchestra. The complexity of making bread depends on the breadmaker and the desired results; but however the bread is made there are several basic steps and ingredients which cannot be avoided. You might say that the actual making of a loaf of bread depends primarily on your palms, your wrists and the hospitable environment in which you are making your loaf. Bread's ingredients enjoy mixing together in a room-temperature climate and dough likes to be kneaded free of air bubbles and develop an ear lobe consistency on a floured wooden board.

The most fundamental unleavened bread, such as Mexico's flat tortilla, is just a combination of flour and water. Most breads that are more familiar to the Western world are leavened breads, which is a way of saying that an activating ingredient, such as yeast or sourdough, is added to make the dough rise and give the bread more body. The Earthbread made in the film is based on a fundamental recipe including these axiomatic ingredients: yeast, water, honey, milk, oil, and whole wheat grains.

Bread Energy

Bread has helped vitalize mankind for thousands of years. Yet today, in the midst of our most impressive technological advancements, we are slowly learning that what is the best is not always the newest. Our preoccupation with uniformity and speed has gradually transformed the energy of bread into an almost impotent food source. By making bread ourselves, and by using whole grains and natural, chemically free ingredients, we can give back to bread its strength. That's simply to say in a whole grain bread which we make, we are getting all the nutrients which are diminished in many commercial processes. Our recent awakening to the environment has shown us dramatically that nature's balance is not to be taken gratuitously.

Bread Recipes

We've selected some bread recipes for you to try. They are not absolute in terms of amounts or ingredients. They are simply a basis for beginning. You can convert any recipe or grandmother's favorite into a whole grain bread formula by taking into account that whole grains are denser and heavier than depleted white flour and less should be used when you are substituting.

When you make bread make it. Neatness does not count. Use your hands, cover them with dough. Use your nose, the aroma of bread is not sold in any aerosol container. And the best part — masticate and savor.

BREAD INGREDIENTS

Flour

Whole grain flours keep ideally in dark, dry, cool places. If you have space in your refrigerator, keep the flours in there. Flours can also be frozen. If you find it difficult to buy the variety of whole grain flour you want in household quantities, you might consider buying the grain you want in larger amounts and grinding your own flour with a small home mill as needed.

Yeast

Yeast is commonly available in two different forms — compressed cakes and dry granules — both come in measured packages. Dry granular yeast keeps for several months in the refrigerator.

To produce whole grain bread which is free of chemical additives, read the ingredients on the labels of the yeast you buy — BHA and BHT are commonly added preservatives.

Dry yeast is also available in large economy amounts, usually in health food stores. Two teaspoons of the dry granules equal: 1 of the pre-measured cakes or packaged dry granules. If you want to make a sourdough bread substitute 2 cups of sourdough starter for 1 package of yeast and slightly reduce the amount of flour you use.

The amount of yeast you use determines how fast your bread rises. On a cool day you may want to add more yeast. No matter how much yeast you put in, the bread should not taste "yeasty" if you punch the dough down at the right time. But remember, the longer your bread rises, with less yeast, the finer the texture will be.

Sweetening

Honey varies in sweetness, but generally can be substituted for sugar on a one to one basis. When proofing yeast be sure to add a bit of honey to get it off to a good start.

Shortening

An equal amount of oil can be substituted for butter or lard in any recipe. Safflower and corn oil are generally the best for bread. If you like a stronger flavor try sesame or soy oil.

Salt

Salt is used only to enhance the flavor. (It can be omitted for those on salt-free diets.) Do not put salt in when you are proofing yeast for the yeast action will be retarded. Add salt with the flour.

Liquid

The water used to dissolve the yeast should be lukewarm, "the temperature of a comfortably hot bath." Milk, reconstituted or powdered, or potato water can be substituted for water. Each produces a slightly different taste, but any of these will improve the texture of your bread.

Additions

There are many different ingredients that can be added to bread to increase its nutritional value and change its taste. If you want to enrich your bread naturally, try using powdered milk, soy flour, wheat germ, rice polishings, your favorite fruits, nuts or seeds.

CONVERTING AND INVENTING RECIPES

Some whole wheat or rye flour is necessary for a yeast dough to rise as both flours contain gluten. A safe ratio is 2 cups of whole wheat or rye for every 1 cup of other flour. Rye loaves will be naturally more compact and moist than wheat.

The addition of soy flour tends to make a loaf of bread brown faster. If you include a substantial amount lower the baking temperature a little (maybe 25 degrees F).

Potato flour tends to lump so blend it with the oil before adding it to the other ingredients.

Oatmeal, or any cooked or soaked cereal, enhances the texture of bread. It also helps the bread stay moist longer. If you substitute cooked cereals for flour you must reduce the liquid. Raw cereals can be soaked in the measured amount of liquid listed in a recipe.

To convert recipes, substitute for each cup of white flour:

> *7/8 cup rice flour*
> *1-1/4 cup rye flour*
> *1 cup rye meal*
> *5/8 cup potato flour*
> *3/4 cup buckwheat flour*
> *7/8 cup cornmeal*
> *1-1/2 cup oatmeal*
> *1/4 cup bean flour*

The balance between flour and liquid will depend on the texture of the flour you use. It will always vary a little even using the same kind of flour with the same recipe. Do not be afraid to keep adding flour to your dough if it seems to need it. But also, do not force too much flour into your dough just because the recipe calls for it. Go by feel. If the dough is springy, with that "ear lobe consistency", stop kneading in flour.

EARTHBREAD

YIELD: 1 large loaf

> *1 cup milk*
> *1 cup water*
> *2 tablespoons yeast*
> *4 tablespoons honey*
> *1 tablespoon oil (corn or safflower)*
> *2 teaspoons salt*
> *1/2 cup wheat germ*
> *4 cups whole wheat flour*
> *Glaze:*
> *1 egg beaten with*
> *1 teaspoon of water*
> *sesame seeds*

Scald milk and set aside to cool.

Dissolve yeast in lukewarm water — "the temperature of a comfortably hot bath" — and add one tablespoon of honey. Set aside to proof. In a large bowl combine lukewarm milk, honey, oil and salt. Add yeast mixture. Stir in two cups of flour. Beat. Add wheat germ then gradually add remaining flour until dough pulls away from the side of the bowl. Turn onto floured board and knead about 10 minutes "until springy and no longer sticky." Place in oiled bowl, cover with a damp cloth and set aside to rise.

When dough has doubled in bulk, punch down and form into a loaf. Place loaf in oiled loaf pan and set aside for second rising. Glaze loaf and bake on the center rack of a preheated (350 degrees F.) oven for 50 minutes.

INDIAN SPOON BREAD

YIELD: 1 medium-sized dish serving 6 to 8

This traditional southern dish traces its name to the Indian porridge, *Suppawn*. It offers a delightful change from bread. It retains the consistency of a porridge or pudding. Discover as Ben Franklin did, "that Indian corn is one of the most agreeable and wholesome grains in the world."

1 cup water-ground corn meal
1 teaspoon salt
2 cups boiling water
1 cup cold milk
4 eggs
5 tablespoons butter, melted

Combine corn meal and salt in mixing bowl. Stir in boiling water till smooth. Let stand for few minutes, then mix in cold milk. Add one egg at a time, beating hard after each addition. Stir in melted butter.

Butter a medium-sized earthenware or glass dish. Pour batter into baking dish and bake for 30 minutes at 425 degrees F. Serve hot with butter.

WHEAT SOURDOUGH ENGLISH MUFFINS

YIELD: 3 dozen muffins

If you like muffins, you'll be intrigued by the wild flavor of these wheat sourdoughs.

1 cup sourdough starter
2 cups milk
5 cups whole wheat flour
2 tablespoons honey
1-1/2 teaspoons salt
2 tablespoons safflower oil
1 tablespoon dry yeast
1/2 cup wheat germ
1/2 cup corn meal

Combine the starter, scalded milk which has cooled down, and 2 cups of whole wheat flour in a large bowl. Cover with plastic wrap and let stand in warm place overnight. (Don't forget to replenish remainder of sourdough starter by adding 1 cup of flour and 1 cup of lukewarm water to the sourdough mixture and return it to the refrigerator.)

In the morning, stir down mixture with wooden spoon. Add honey, salt, oil and yeast. Add wheat germ and the remainder of the flour, except 1/2 cup for kneading. Turn onto a lightly floured board and knead till smooth, about 10 minutes. Sprinkle flour board with corn meal and roll out dough to 3/8-inch thickness. Cut with large, round cutter and let rise for an hour.

Fry the muffins on a preheated griddle at 275 degrees F. for 15 minutes on each side. Turn only once and be careful not to burn.

Serve split and toasted.

JACK OF ALL BREADS
YIELD: 1 Challah loaf, 3 dozen rolls, 2 pizza

If you don't have much time to knead, this may well become your favorite bread recipe. This no-knead dough is a basic one for Challah, pizza dough, hamburger rolls, or hearty crescent rolls. It can be stirred up in half an hour, then refrigerated overnight.

4 teaspoons dry yeast
1 cup lukewarm spring water
3-1/3 tablespoons honey
1 cup safflower oil
2 teaspoons salt
1 cup boiling water
1/2 cup wheat germ
2 eggs, beaten
5-1/2 cups whole wheat flour

Dissolve yeast in lukewarm water. Add 1 teaspoon honey. In large bowl, mix oil, 3 tablespoons honey, salt and boiling water. Add wheat germ when mixture is lukewarm, add eggs, then dissolved yeast. Gradually stir in whole wheat flour, mixing well. Do not knead. Put in refrigerator to chill till firm.

JACK OF ALL BREADS VARIATION:
Whole Wheat Crescent Rolls

YIELD: 3 dozen rolls

For egg glaze:
  1 egg, beaten
  1/4 teaspoon water
  4 tablespoons sesame or poppy seeds

Divide dough into three parts and roll each part out thinly on a floured board into a large circle. Brush with beaten egg to which the water has been added. Sprinkle toasted sesame seeds or poppy seeds over the surface. Cut each circle into wedges about 2 inches wide at the outside edge. Roll each wedge toward the center, lift off the board, dip top in egg mixture, and then in sesame seeds or poppy seeds.

Place on an oiled cookie sheet, leaving enough room for each crescent to rise. Let rise for one hour. Bake in preheated oven at 425 degrees F. for 25 minutes until golden brown. Serve warm.

JACK OF ALL BREADS VARIATION:
Whole Wheat Herb Rolls

YIELD: 3 dozen rolls

Proceed in the same way as above, spreading freshly picked, chopped herbs such as parsley, marjoram, thyme, basil, oregano, and dill on top of egg glaze. Then roll wedges toward the center and shape into crescent rolls. Glaze and sprinkle with toasted sesame seeds.

JACK OF ALL BREADS VARIATION:

Poppy Seed Twist Loaf

YIELD: 1 large loaf

For egg glaze:
> 1 egg, beaten
> 1/4 teaspoon water
> 1/2 cup poppy seeds

Divide the basic dough into three parts. Roll out each part on a floured board. Then shape into three fat, long coils of dough. Braid these into a large loaf. Glaze with egg glaze, and sprinkle liberally with poppy seeds.

Place on a large, oiled cookie sheet to rise for an hour.

Bake in preheated oven at 425-degrees F. for 25 minutes till deep brown. Let cool on wire racks. Serve warm.

JACK OF ALL BREADS VARIATION:

Whole Wheat Buns

YIELD: 3 dozen buns

For egg glaze:
> 1 beaten egg
> 1/4 teaspoon water
> 4 tablespoons sesame seeds

Roll out the basic dough on floured board. Make hamburger-sized buns using a large round cutter. Glaze with egg glaze and sprinkle with toasted sesame seeds.

Place buns on an oiled cookie sheet to rise for an hour.

Bake in preheated oven at 425 degrees F. for 25 minutes till golden brown. Let cool on wire racks. Serve warm.

JACK OF ALL BREADS VARIATION:

Pizza Dough

YIELD: 3 pizzas

Roll out the basic dough and place in square baking pans. Place tomatoes on top of the dough and bake in a preheated oven at 500-degrees F. for 15 minutes.

Take out the pizza dough and place more tomatoes and mozzarella cheese on it. Replace in the oven to cook for 10 more minutes at 500-degrees F.

IRISH RAISIN BREAD

YIELD: 2 round loaves

Around Ireland's Dingle Bay, where this traditional yeast bread originates, it is known as "Curranty Cake." The flavors of oatmeal and stone ground whole wheat flour mingle with raisins, imparting a nutty taste.

8 teaspoons dry yeast
2 cups warm spring water
4 tablespoons honey
1/2 cup skim milk powder
1/2 cup safflower oil
1-1/2 teaspoons salt
1/2 cup wheat germ
2 eggs, well-beaten
2 cups oatmeal
6 cups whole wheat flour, warmed
1 cup raisins or currants
For egg glaze:
1 egg beaten with 1/2 teaspoon water

Dissolve yeast in 1 cup warm spring water. Add 1 tablespoon of the honey to proof. Combine skim milk powder with the remaining water and heat. Add oil, salt, wheat germ, and remaining honey.

In a large mixing bowl, combine milk mixture, eggs, and yeast mixture. Mix in the oatmeal and 5-1/2 cups of the whole wheat flour, a cup at a time. Reserve the other 1/2 cup for kneading. Knead till smooth and elastic, for about 10 minutes. Put in an oiled bowl. Cover with a damp towel and let rise till double in size, approximately 1-1/2 hours.

Stir dough down and knead with remaining flour, gradually working in the raisins or currants. Shape into two round loaves. Brush with egg glaze. Put loaves on oiled cookie sheets to rise for an hour.

Bake in preheated oven at 375 degrees F. for 25 minutes or till golden brown. Remove from pan onto wire racks.

WHOLE WHEAT SOFT PRETZELS

YIELD: 16 pretzels

> *2-1/2 cups very warm water*
> *1 teaspoon honey*
> *2 teaspoons yeast*
> *1 teaspoon salt*
> *5 cups whole wheat flour*

Egg glaze:
> *whole egg beaten with 1/4 teaspoon water;*
> *coarse salt to taste*

Combine water, honey, yeast. Let sit for one hour. Add the salt and flour — just enough to make a fairly soft dough. Knead thoroughly.

Let rise until double in bulk, about 45 minutes
to one hour. Punch down. Pinch off pieces of
dough, golf ball-sized, roll into long cylinders
and shape into pretzels (fat ones). Place on a
greased cookie sheet. Brush them with egg glaze
and sprinkle with coarse salt. Bake in preheated
oven at 450 degrees F. for 15 minutes. Cool on
a rack.

TUTTIFRUIT QUICKBREAD

YIELD: 1 loaf

Here's a kaleidoscope of dried fruit and nut
colors and flavors mingling into this light, high-
rising quickbread. You may have tried quick-
breads, but none taste so grand as this one —
made with stone ground whole wheat flour and
wheat germ and with fresh lemon, orange rind
and nutmeg.

3 cups whole wheat flour
1/4 cup wheat germ
1/2 teaspoon salt
4 teaspoons baking powder
2 teaspoons nutmeg
1/2 cup ground walnuts or other nutmeats
1 cup chopped dates, raisins, prunes, or figs
2 eggs, well beaten
1/2 cup honey
1-1/2 cups milk or buttermilk

Mix the dry ingredients, using 1 teaspoon of the
nutmeg, and toss the dried chopped fruits and
nuts through them. Reserve 1 teaspoon of the
nutmeats.

Combine the beaten eggs, honey, and milk.
Beat. Make a well in the center of the flour and
add the egg mixture, mixing thoroughly.

Butter a loaf pan. Place 1 teaspoon nutmeg, combined with 1 teaspoon ground nuts on the top for decoration before baking. Bake in pre-heated oven set at 350 degrees F. for 50 minutes.

SWEDISH RYE

YIELD: 3 round loaves

> *3 cups warm water*
> *2 tablespoons yeast*
> *1/2 cup honey*
> *1/2 cup molasses*
> *1-1/2 teaspoons anise*
> *2 teaspoons grated orange peel*
> *6 cups (approx.) whole wheat flour*
> *1/2 cup oil*
> *1 tablespoon salt*
> *4 cups rye flour*
> *sprinkle of corn meal*

Combine water, yeast, honey and molasses. Let sit for about five minutes until the yeast rises to the surface. Add anise, orange peel, 3 cups whole wheat flour. Stir thoroughly. Let rise 15 to 30 minutes. Stir down. Add the oil, salt, rye flour, and enough whole wheat flour to make a fairly stiff dough. Knead thoroughly. Let rise until doubled in bulk, usually about one hour. Punch down. Shape into three round loaves. Place on cookie sheet sprinkled with corn meal. Cut a slit in the top of each. Let rise until almost double, around 1/2 hour. Bake at 375 degrees F. about 40 minutes or until done. Cool on a rack.

OLD COUNTRY PUMPERNICKEL
YIELD: 2 round loaves

The Germans who settled in many parts of our country brought with them the Westphalian peasant bread we know as pumpernickel. This old country recipe has little resemblance to its weak rye cousin sold in supermarkets.

2 large potatoes, water to cover
2 teaspoons dry yeast
1 teaspoon honey
3 cups cold water
3/4 cup corn meal
1/2 cup molasses
1/2 cup caraway seeds
2 tablespoons safflower oil
4 teaspoons salt
5 cups rye flour
1/2 cup wheat germ
6 cups whole wheat flour

For egg glaze:
1 beaten egg
1/4 teaspoon water

Cook potatoes in enough water to cover. Drain, save 1/2 cup potato water. Push potatoes through strainer or ricer while still hot. Measure 2 cups potatoes into bowl and leave to cool.

Soften yeast in lukewarm potato water. Add honey and let stand for 5 minutes.

Combine 3 cups cold water and corn meal and boil, stirring constantly till thick. Add molasses, 1 tablespoon of the caraway seeds, oil and salt to corn meal mixture. Let mixture cool to lukewarm. Add the riced potatoes and all of yeast mixture to lukewarm corn meal mixture and blend well.

Add rye flour gradually, then wheat germ and wheat flour, reserving enough to knead with. Knead thoroughly, about 15 minutes. Place in large, oiled bowl to rise. Cover with a damp towel. Allow 2-1/2 hours for rising.

Punch down and shape into two round loaves. Glaze with beaten egg-water mixture. Prick tops with fork design. Sprinkle remaining caraway seeds on top of loaves. Oil a cookie sheet and sprinkle it with corn meal. Place on cookie sheet and allow to rise for one hour.

Bake in preheated oven at 375 degrees F. for 45 minutes.

DESSERTS

DATE TREATS
YIELD: 4 DOZEN

> 1 pound pitted dates
> 1/4 cup old-fashioned peanut butter
> 1/2 cup chopped pecans or walnuts

Mix peanut butter with chopped nuts and fill cavity of dates.

GRANOLA CANDY
YIELD: 2 DOZEN PIECES

> 1/2 cup old fashioned peanut butter
> 1/2 cup raw honey
> 1/2 cup granola or crushed wheat flakes
> 1/4 cup non-instant dry milk powder

Combine the peanut butter with the honey. Add the granola and the milk powder. Roll into a long roll. Chill until firm. Slice.

NUT BUTTER CANDY

> 1/4 cup old fashioned peanut butter
> 1/2 cup pecan halves, ground
> 2 tablespoons raw honey
> 2 tablespoons non instant milk powder
> Optional: ground nuts or coconut for
>   rolling candy in

Mix all ingredients well. Roll into small balls. The amount of milk powder may be increased to make the mix firm enough to roll. Roll the balls in ground nuts or coconut if desired. Chill. Try other nut butters and nuts for variety.

NUTTY CHEWS
YIELD: 1 DOZEN

1/2 cup wheat sprouts
1/2 cup almonds or other nuts
1/2 cup raisins
1/8 teaspoon sea salt

Grind all the ingredients together. Shape into small balls. The sprouts are sweetest when short, about 1/4 inch long including the grain.

BUENUELLOS

whole wheat flour tortillas, cut into fourths
unrefined safflower oil for deep frying
maple syrup or raw honey
cinnamon

Fry tortilla pieces in hot oil. Drain on paper. Drizzle with syrup or honey. Sprinkle with cinnamon.

DATE BALLS

2 cups pitted dates
1 cup dried figs
1/2 cup raisins
1-1/2 cups chopped pecans

Put dates, figs, and raisins through grinder. Stir in chopped nuts. Mix well. Shape into small balls and roll in grated coconut   or finely chopped nuts. Store in air-tight container.

PEANUT BUTTER BALLS

1/2 cup raw honey
1/2 cup old-fashioned peanut butter
3/4 wheat germ
3/4 cup milk powder

Mix all ingredients well. Roll into small balls. Roll in ground nuts if desired. Chill.

BACKPACK SNACK

wheat or rye flakes
sesame seeds
sunflower seeds
whole or chopped nuts
raisins
dried fruits, chopped

Toast the flakes, sesame seeds, and sunflower seeds in an ungreased skillet. Pour into a bowl and mix with nutmeats, raisins, and any desired chopped dried fruits. Cool the mixture completely. Carry in tightly closed plastic bags or other containers.

HONEY NUTS

6 ounces, shelled raw nuts (unsalted)
1 tablespoon melted butter
1 tablespoon raw honey

Spread nuts on cookie sheet and toast in oven 15 minutes at 300 degrees. Mix butter and honey with the hot nuts. Spread out and cool.

CAMPERS' CAKE

1- 8 x 8 CAKE

2 cups whole wheat flour
3 tablespoons carob powder (optional)
2 teaspoons low sodium baking powder
1/2 teaspoon sea salt
1 tablespoon vanilla
4 tablespoons unrefined oil
1 tablespoon apple cider vinegar
1/2 cup raw honey
1 cup very warm apple juice or coffee type drink

Mix the dry ingredients in ungreased 8 x 8 inch cake pan. Make 3 holes in the dry mix. Put vanilla in one, oil in one, and vinegar in one. Dissolve the honey in the juice. Pour this liquid

over the mix. Stir all in the pan until smooth.
Bake 30 minutes at 350 degrees. Spread with
one of the simple fruit fillings, syrups, or yogurt
dessert sauce.

PLAIN CAKE

2 cups whole wheat pastry flour
3 teaspoons low sodium baking powder
1 teaspoon sea salt
1/2 cup unrefined safflower oil
1/2 cup raw honey
1 cup milk
2 eggs
2 teaspoons vanilla

Mix dry ingredients. Add oil, honey and half the
milk and beat with a spoon 1 or 2 minutes. Add
remaining ingredients and beat again. Pour into
an ungreased 9 x 13 inch pan. Bake 30 to 35
minutes at 350 degrees. Serve with a simple
syrup, sauce or yogurt icing.

POUND CAKE

1 cup butter, softened
3/4 cup raw honey
juice and grated rind of one lemon
4 eggs
1/4 teaspoon low-sodium baking powder
1 1/4 cups whole wheat pastry flour

Cream the butter and honey for five minutes.
Add the lemon juice. Add the eggs, beating well.
Mix the baking powder and flour. Stir into the
egg mixture until well mixed. Pour into oiled
loaf pan. Bake 75 minutes at 300 degrees.

QUICK COBBLER
SERVES 6

> 6 tablespoons butter
> 1-1/2 cups whole wheat flour
> 1/4 teaspoon sea salt
> 1 teaspoon low sodium baking powder
> 1/2 cup raw honey
> 1 egg, beaten
> 1 cup milk
> 2 cups fresh fruit, with 1/4 cup more raw
>   honey if fruit is tart

Melt the butter in 1-1/2 quart flat baking dish in the oven. Mix the flour, salt, baking powder, honey, egg, and milk. Pour in the center of the melted butter in the dish. Pour the fruit over the top. Bake 30 to 35 minutes at 400 degrees.

ALMOND FILLING OR ICING

> 2/3 cup milk
> 4 tablespoons raw honey
> 2 tablespoons whole wheat flour
> 1 cup finely chopped almonds

Mix all ingredients except nuts in a small pan. Cook over low heat stirring constantly until thick. Stir in nuts and cool.

APPLESAUCE FILLING or ICING ·

> 1 cup thick applesauce
> 2 teaspoons lemon juice
> 2 tablespoons whole wheat flour
> 6 tablespoons raw honey

Mix all ingredients in a small pan. Cook stirring constantly on low heat until thick. Cool.

DATE FILLING

> 1-1/2 cups chopped dates or figs
> 2/3 cup apple juice
> 2 tablespoons raw honey
> 2 tablespoons lemon juice
> 1-1/2 cups finely chopped nuts

✂ Mix all ingredients in a small pan. Cook over low heat stirring constantly until thick. Cool.

VANILLA CREAM FILLING or ICING

> 1 cup milk
> 2 tablespoons whole wheat flour
> 2 eggs, beaten
> 4 tablespoons raw honey
> 4 teaspoons vanilla

✂ Mix all ingredients in a small pan. Cook over low heat, stirring constantly until thick. Cool and stir in vanilla.

APPLE SYRUP
YIELD: 1-1/2 cups

> 3 cups apple juice, boiled down to 1½ cups
> 2 tablespoons butter
> 2 tablespoons whole wheat flour

✂ Melt the butter on low heat. Stir in the flour. Gradually add the boiled down apple juice, stirring constantly. Raise heat until mixture almost simmers, but do not allow it to boil. Cook, stirring constantly until the sauce thickens, about 5 minutes. This sauce is good on pancakes or spooned over a plain cake.

SYRUP SAUCE

YIELD: 1-1/2 cups

> 1-1/2 cups pure maple syrup or unsulphered
>   molasses
> 3 tablespoons butter
> 3 tablespoons lemon juice

✧ Mix all well. Simmer 5 to 10 minutes.

YOGURT DESSERT FONDUE SAUCE

YIELD: 1 CUP

> 1/2 cup plain yogurt
> 1/4 cup mild raw honey
> 1/3 cup non instant milk powder
> 1 tablespoon vanilla
> juice of 1/2 lime
> Optional: 1 tablespoon butter

✧ Beat or blend all the ingredients well. Chill.
Thin with a little apple juice if necessary before
serving.
Prepare fresh fruits for dipping. Strawberries
pineapple, banana and apple pieces are good. Be
sure to coat the banana and apple slices with
lemon or lime juice to prevent darkening.
To use as an icing: Include the butter and add
enough more milk powder to make the icing
thick but spreadable.

APRICOT SQUARES

YIELD: (16 squares)

> 1-1/2 cups chopped dried apricots (about
>   8 ounces)
> 2 cups water
> 1/4 cup raw honey
> 1-1/2 cups oat flakes
> 1-1/2 cups whole wheat pastry flour

1/2 cup chopped walnuts
1/2 cup unrefined safflower oil
1/2 cup raw honey

Mix the apricots, water, and honey in a saucepan. Bring to a boil and simmer uncovered on low heat for 10 minutes. Mix the flakes, flour, nuts, oil, and honey. Press half of this mixture in the bottom of an 8 x 8 inch pan. Spread the cooked apricot mixture over the flake crust. Sprinkle the remaining flake mix over the top. Bake 20 to 30 minutes at 350 degrees until lightly browned. Cool and cut into 16 squares.

BUTTERSCOTCH COOKIES

1/4 cup unrefined oil
2 tablespoons dark molasses
1/2 cup raw honey
2 eggs
2 teaspoons vanilla
1/2 cup chopped nuts
1 cup wheat germ
1 cup whole wheat flour
1/4 teaspoon sea salt

Mix liquid ingredients. Add nuts. Stir in wheat germ, flour and salt. Drop by teaspoonful on an oiled cookie sheet. Bake 15 minutes at 350 degrees.

CREAM CHEESE COOKIES

YIELD: 2 DOZEN

1/4 cup raw honey
1/4 cup unrefined oil
1/2 cup cream cheese or yogurt cream cheese
1 cup whole wheat flour
1/4 teaspoon sea salt
3 tablespoons sesame seeds or poppy seeds

✄ Blend honey and oil with cheese. Add flour, salt and seeds. Roll dough into a long roll. Wrap in wax paper. Chill and cut into thin slices. Bake on oiled cookie sheet 5 to 8 minutes at 400 degrees.

GRANOLA COOKIES
YIELD: 3 to 4 DOZEN COOKIES

> *1 cup unrefined safflower oil*
> *3/4 cup raw honey*
> *2 eggs*
> *1 cup sunflower seeds or chopped nuts*
> *1 teaspoon vanilla*
> *2 cups whole wheat flour*
> *1/2 teaspoon sea salt*
> *2-1/2 cups Maple Nut Granola*

✄ Mix oil, honey, eggs, nuts, and vanilla. Add flour and salt. Stir in Granola. Mix well and drop by teaspoon on to cookie sheet. Bake at 300 degrees for 15 to 20 minutes.

GRANOLA MACAROONS

> *3 tablespoons raw honey*
> *dash of sea salt*
> *1 egg, well beaten*
> *1/4 cup wholewheat flour*
> *1 cup grated coconut*
> *1 cup Maple Nut Granola*

✄ Combine all ingredients. Drop by spoonfuls on oiled baking sheet. Bake 12 minutes at 325 degrees or until slightly brown.

HONEY COOKIES

YIELD: 3 dozen

> *1/2 cup raw honey*
> *1/2 cup unrefined oil*
> *1 egg, beaten*
> *2 teaspoons vanilla*
> *1 cup whole wheat flour or whole wheat pastry*
>   *flour*

Mix the liquid ingredients. Stir in flour to make stiff dough, adding fruit juice or more flour to give proper consistency. Drop by teaspoonfuls on oiled cookie sheet. Leave room for cookies to spread out. Bake 12 to 15 minutes at 375 degrees until edges of cookies are brown.

OATMEAL COOKIES

YIELD: 3 DOZEN

> *1/2 cup raw honey*
> *1 tablespoon unrefined oil*
> *2 eggs, beaten*
> *grated rind of one lemon*
> *1/2 teaspoon sea salt*
> *2 cups oatmeal*
> *1/2 cup whole wheat flour*

Mix all ingredients together to make a stiff dough. If too thick add a little milk. Drop by teaspoonfuls onto an oiled cookie sheet. Bake 8 to 10 minutes at 400 degrees.

OATMEAL BANANA COOKIES

YIELD: 4 DOZEN

> *2 cups oat flakes*
> *2 cups whole wheat flour*
> *3/4 cup oil*
> *3/4 cup chopped nuts*

> 3/4 cup raisins
> 2 bananas, mashed
> 1 cup apple juice

Mix flakes and flour. Stir in oil evenly. Add remaining ingredients. Add a little flour if necessary to stiffen dough. Drop onto oiled cookie sheet and bake about 30 minutes at 350 degrees.

OATMEAL SHORTBREAD

YIELD: 12 SQUARES

> 3½ cups oatmeal
> 1/4 cup whole wheat flour
> 1/2 teaspoon sea salt
> 1/3 cup unrefined oil
> 1/3 cup raw honey
> 1 teaspoon vanilla

Mix all ingredients together to make a stiff dough. Press dough into an oiled and floured 9 x 13 inch pan. Bake until light brown, about 30 minutes at 325 degrees. Cool 10 minutes. Cut into squares. Serve with fruit.

SESAME SQUARES

> 1 cup whole wheat flour
> 1 cup soy flour
> 1½ cups sesame seeds
> ¼ cup almonds, chopped
> ½ teaspoon sea salt
> 3/4 cup raw honey
> 3/4 cup unrefined oil

Mix all ingredients together, adding a little milk if necessary to make stiff dough. Roll thin, cut in squares and place on oiled sheet. Bake at 350 degrees until golden brown.

PEANUT BUTTER COOKIES

YIELD: 2 to 3 DOZEN

> 1/3 cup unrefined peanut oil
> 1/2 cup raw honey
> 2/3 cup old fashioned peanut butter
> 1 egg, well beaten
> 1-1/2 cups whole wheat flour, sifted

Beat the oil and honey well. Add the egg and peanut butter and beat. Add the flour and just mix. Drop by the teaspoonful on an oiled cookie sheet. Bake 7 to 10 minutes at 400 degrees. Watch carefully. Do not overcook. Children enjoy making these simple cookies.

RICE FLOUR COOKIES

YIELD: 2 DOZEN

> 1 cup brown rice flour
> 1/2 cup unrefined oil
> 4 tablespoons raw honey
> 1 teaspoon vanilla
> 1 egg, slightly beaten
> 1 cup nuts, ground

Blend all ingredients thoroughly. Cover and chill overnight. Roll into balls the size of walnuts. Arrange on a well oiled cookie sheet. Press flat with the bottom of a glass. Bake about 12 minutes at 350 degrees.

WHEAT GERM COOKIES

YIELD: 4 DOZEN

> 3 eggs, well beaten
> 1 cup raw honey
> 2/3 cup unrefined safflower oil
> 2 teaspoons vanilla

    2 cups whole wheat pastry flour
    1 cup wheat germ
    1 cup soy flour
    pinch of sea salt

>⊂◗ Mix liquid ingredients. Mix and add dry ingredi-
       ents. Drop by teaspoon on oiled baking sheet
       and bake at 350 degrees till done.

FRUIT YOGURT

SERVES 6

    2 cups plain yogurt
    2 cups finely chopped fresh fruit
    raw honey to taste

>⊂◗ Mix all ingredients and chill. If desired, freeze to
      a soft mush. Stir well and freeze to ice cream.

BAKED APPLES

SERVES 4

    4 large apples
    1/2 cup boiling water
    raw honey
    cinnamon
    nutmeg

>⊂◗ Peel upper 1/3 of apples and core. Put peeled
       side down. Add boiling water. Cover and heat
       quickly. Reduce heat and simmer 10 minutes
       or until tender. Turn right side up. Drizzle with
       raw honey. Sprinkle with cinnamon or nutmeg.
       Serve with milk or cream.

BAKED APRICOTS

    Whole fresh apricots, nectarines, peaches or
        other fruit
    Raw honey

⤛ Wash fruit but do not peel. Preheat a heavy pan. Add a few tablespoons of water. Add fruit. Cover and steam until tender, about 5 to 10 minutes, depending on the size of the fruit. Remove skins if desired. Drizzle fruit with honey. Cool.

DRIED APPLE APPLESAUCE
YIELD: 2 CUPS

> *6 ounces dried apples*
> *2 cups water*
> *1 teaspoon lemon juice*
> *Optional: raw honey to taste*

⤛ Simmer the apples in the water until very soft. Add the lemon juice and honey if desired. Serve as is or put through a food mill.

CHUNKY OVEN APPLESAUCE

> *12 apples*
> *1/2 teaspoon cinnamon*
> *1/4 teaspoon sea salt*
> *1/8 teaspoon nutmeg*
> *1/4 cup raw honey*
> *1/4 cup water*
> *2-3 tablespoons butter*

⤛ Core the apples. Cut them into wedges. Place the wedges in a buttered baking dish. Mix spices together and sprinkle them over the apples. Drizzle the honey over the apples. Dot with butter. Add the water. Cover and bake 1 to 1-1/2 hours at 300 degrees.

APPLE CRISP

  1 pound sliced apples
  1 cup whole wheat pastry flour
  1/2 cup unrefined oil
  1/4 cup honey
  1 cup raisins

Arrange a layer of sliced apples in bottom of well oiled baking dish. Mix remaining ingredients and cover apples with a layer of mixture. Repeat layers. Bake until golden and sizzling, about 40 minutes at 350 degrees.

HONEY RHUBARB

SERVES 4 to 6

  4 cups 1/2" pieces of rhubarb
  1/2 cup raw honey
  1 teaspoon nutmeg
  1/8 teaspoon sea salt
  2 tablespoons milk or water
  4 tablespoons melted butter
  1/2 cup raw honey
  4 cups cubed whole wheat bread

Mix the rhubarb, honey, nutmeg, salt and milk or water. Pour into a flat 10 x 6 inch baking dish. Mix the butter and honey and then add the bread cubes. Pour the honeyed cubes over the rhubarb mixture. Bake 30 minutes at 375 degrees or until golden.

NOODLE PIE
1-9" PIE

> 2 cups cooked whole wheat noodles
> 2 cups grated fresh apple or cooked dried apples
> 1/4 to 1/2 cup raw honey
> 2 teaspoons cinnamon
> 2 to 4 tablespoons cream

Spread the cooked noodles in an oiled pie plate.
Spread the apples over the noodles. Drizzle with
honey and cream. Sprinkle with cinnamon.
Bake 20 to 30 minutes at 350 degrees.

PIE DOUGH
2 - 9" PIE SHELLS

> 2-1/2 cups whole wheat pastry flour
> 1/2 teaspoon sea salt
> 1/3 cup unrefined corn germ oil
> 1/3 cup water

Mix all ingredients lightly with a fork. Cut the
dough in half and roll out between 2 sheets of
waxed paper.

CRUMB CRUSTS

I. *1 cup shredded coconut*
    1/2 cup wheat germ
    2 tablespoons soft butter

Mix well. Press into 9 inch pie plate. Chill before filling.

II. *1 cup crushed wheat flakes, crushed granola, cake*
        or cookie crumbs
    1/2 cup wheat germ
    1/3 cup unrefined oil

Mix all ingredients. Add a tablespoon of honey
if flakes are used. Press into a 9 inch pie plate.
Chill before filling.

CUSTARD

   4 cups fresh milk, or reconstituted powdered
      milk with 4 tablespoons butter
   4 to 6 eggs, beaten well
   1/4 cup raw honey
   pinch of sea salt

Mix all ingredients together well in a heavy
saucepan. Cook over medium heat, stirring
constantly, until custard coats metal spoon and
begins to steam. Do not allow to boil. Remove
from heat. Cool and stir in 3 teaspoons vanilla.

INDIAN PUDDING

SERVES 8

   1 cup stone ground cornmeal
   1/2 cup whole wheat flour
   7 cups cold water
   1/4 cup unrefined safflower oil
   3/4 cup raw honey
   1/2 teaspoon cinnamon

Mix cornmeal and flour. Stir in cold water.
Bring to boil and simmer till very thick. Add oil,
honey and cinnamon and stir. Serve hot or cold.

CRACKED WHEAT PUDDING

SERVES 6

   1 quart milk
   1-1/2 cups cracked wheat or bulghur or bulghur-
      soy grits
   1/2 teaspoon sea salt
   4 tablespoons raw honey
   1/2 cup raisins
   1/4 teaspoon nutmeg

><Bring milk to boil in top of double broiler over direct heat. Stir in remaining ingredients. Place pan over bottom of double boiler containing hot water. Cover. Continue to cook over low heat until thick and all liquid is absorbed. Serve hot topped with yogurt and fruit.

WHEAT-SPROUT PUDDING
SERVES 6

> 1 cup sprouted wheat
> 1/2 cup whole wheat flour
> 1 cup chopped, pitted dates
> 2 cups water
> 1 cup chopped pecans

><Mix all ingredients. Pour into an oiled casserole dish. Bake about 1 hour at 325 degrees: Serve hot or cold topped with fresh fruit.

RICE OR WHOLE WHEAT BERRY PUDDING
SERVES 6

> 3 cups cooked whole wheat berries or cooked
>   brown rice
> 3 cups milk
> 3 eggs, beaten
> 4 tablespoons raw honey or molasses
> 1 cup raisins or chopped fruit
> 1 tablespoon lemon or orange rind
> pinch of sea salt
> pinch of ground mace, cinnamon, or nutmeg
> 1 cup chopped nuts

><Mix all ingredients except nuts. Simmer 30 minutes. Add a little honey to taste. Stir in pecans. Serve hot or chilled.

DATE NUT COOKIES

1 cup whole wheat flour
3 cups rolled oats
1 cup chopped dates
1 cup chopped pecans, walnuts, or almonds
1/4 tsp. salt
1/4 cup safflower, sesame, or sunflower oil
    (unrefined)
1 to 1¼ cups apple juice

In a pan, dry roast the flour over a low flame for about five minutes. Stir frequently. After the flour has cooled, mix all the dry ingredients in a bowl, including the dates and nuts. Add the oil and apple juice. Stir well. The batter should have a moist but firm consistency so that it can be molded in your hand. If the batter is too dry, add more juice; if too wet, add more flour. Roll into small balls about 1-inch in diameter and set on a lightly oiled cookie sheet in rows 1 inch apart. Flatten each cookie with a spoon or fork. Bake at 350 degrees for 20 to 30 minutes.

PARTY KANTEN

SERVES 10 PEOPLE

1½ cups water
9 cups apple juice
3-3½ bars of Agar Agar
2-3 cups fresh sliced fruit (canteloupe,
    strawberries, apples, peaches, pears,
    cherries)

In a large bowl, break up the Agar into small pieces. Add 1-1/2 cups of water and let soak for 5 to 10 minutes. Transfer to a saucepan and bring to a boil. Let boil for five minutes. Lower flame to medium temperature and stir in apple juice. Cook on medium low flame for 15 minutes (at this point mixture will still be very "liquid"). Pour out into shallow dishes and add the fresh fruit (a mixture of any one or all of the above). Let cool to room temperature, then place in refrigerator until it gels. This recipe served as dessert for over 10 people at a Food For Life outing.

*One good lick deserves another — try mixing equal amounts of yogurt and slightly thawed frozen orange juice concentrate. Freeze in ice cube trays with popsicle sticks inserted.

The following six recipes come from the people at Laurelbrook Foods, Bel Air, Maryland.

CRESCENT COOKIES

1 cup ground nuts
3/4 cup unrefined oil
2-1/2 cups whole wheat flour
1/3 cup honey or sorghum molasses
1 teaspoon vanilla
1 tablespoon Pero dissolved in a little water

Mix together, form into crescents. Bake at 350 degrees till brown. Let cool on cookie sheet.

PEANUT BUTTER COOKIES

1/2 cup unrefined corn oil
1 cup peanut butter
1/2 tsp. sea salt
1-1/2 cups pastry flour
1/2 cup raisins
1-1/2 cups water

Cook the raisins in the 1-1/2 cups water. Blend all ingredients together. Shape into balls and squash with fork. Bake at 375 degrees for 15 minutes.

APPLE CRISP

Roll apple slices in salt, oil, then brown rice flour. Place in baking pan, and cover halfway with apple juice. Sprinkle with golden brown roasted oats, flour and corn oil. Work the oil in to make a crumbly consistency. Bake in 350 degree oven for 1 hour until apple juice bubbles. Crust should be hard and crisp, bottom creamy.

LISA'S LICKS

3/4 cup yogurt
1 tablespoon honey
1/2 tsp. vanilla
Dash nutmeg
1/2 tsp. brewers yeast
Apple juice

Mix together and place in bottom third of popsicle tray. Fill remainder of the tray with apple juice. Freeze

SWITCHEL (Harvest Drink)

1 teaspoon ginger, powdered or grated
2 tablespoons undiluted cider vinegar
1/2 cup honey
1 quart water

Mix all together. Serve with ice. Part apple juice can be substituted for some of the water. Very refreshing on a hot day. Vary the amounts of the ingredients to taste.

CAROB BARS

1/2 cup sunflower seeds 1/4 cup carob powder
1/4 cup peanut butter 1/4 cup rice flakes
1/4 cup sesame seeds Honey

Mix all ingredients together. adding enough honey to make it workable, but not too soft. Shape into bars. It is ready to eat.

EDIBLE
WILD FOODS

Did you know that the little dry pods which form on wild rose bushes after the delicate little roses have dried up and the petals have fallen to the ground can be picked and stored all winter? Did you know that they could be munched on, ground into powder, or brewed into tea? Most importantly, did you know that these little rosehips are perhaps 50 times as rich in vitamin C as some citrus juices? It has been estimated by some historians that scurvy, caused by vitamin C deficiency, has killed many millions of people. Most of these deaths occurred in winter or on board ships at sea. These deaths could have easily been prevented had people known to have a few little bags of rosehips around.

Many people, caught in the wilderness without adequate food supplies of their own, have been saved from starvation because they knew that the sappy layer under the bark of an aspen or a cottonwood tree was edible, or that the fruit of a prickly pear or yucca could make a tasty snack. In the hardwood forests, hickory nuts, native pecans, acorns, black walnuts and other nutritious nuts abound. In the coniferous forests, pinon pine nuts can keep you going. Wild cherries, plums and apples, along with blackberries, raspberries and gooseberries provide a good selection in some parts of the country. The leaves of wild strawberries and grapes can be eaten as well as the fruit.

In the desert, a barrel cactus has quenched the thirst of more than one dry traveler, and chia seeds are famed for their nutritional value. In the swamps, wild rice is a delicacy which brings high prices when it can be found in specialty markets. From the ocean, Irish moss, dulse, laver and kelp are rich in many minerals essential for good health. In middle-America, the sunflower provides good nibbling. Jerusalem artichokes and cattails are widespread and very nutritional.

Mint tea has refreshed many thirsty folks, and a few leaves of mint are good in almost any fruit juice or tea. Watercress is good, either raw or cooked, and a surprising number of "weeds" can be counted on to sustain life or provide a fresh salad in a pinch. These include dandelion, lamb's quarter, pokeweed, clover, mustard, shepherd's purse, chickweed and mountain sorrel. Some are best steeped in hot water a few times, but can be eaten in many ways, and can almost always be improved by a bit of horseradish or a few wild onions.

There are precautions that should be taken if one is going to munch on wild foods which might not be familiar to the muncher. Hard shiny berries should be avoided unless one knows about them, for instance, and wild onions should smell like onions as there are similar plants in appearance which might be toxic. There are many good books on the subject, and one of the most authoritative is Edible Wild Plants, by Oliver Perry Medsger (see recommended books). Most Americans have been over-protected from the real world by a very fragile world of technology. God placed many good things at our disposal on this earth, and you might never know in advance when He might require you to know something about them. John the Baptist did very well.

RECOMMENDED BOOKS & PUBLICATIONS

Angier, Bradford, Skills for Taming the Wilds, (New York: Simon and Schuster, 1972).

Ford, Hillyard & Koock, The Deaf Smith Country Cookbook, (New York: Macmillian Publishing Co. Inc., 1973).

Hunter, Beatrice Trum, Natural Foods Primer, (New York: Simon & Schuster, 1972).

Hurd, Frank & Rosalie, Ten Talents. Write: Collegedale Distributors, Box 626, Collegedale, Tenn. 37315.

Jaeger, Ellsworth, Wildwood Wisdom, (New York: Macmillian Publishing Co., Inc., 1945).

Medsger, Oliver, Edible Wild Plants, (New York: Macmillian Publishing Co., Inc., 1972).

Lappe, Francis Moore, Diet for a Small Planet, (New York: Ballantine Books, 1971).

Summers, Bob, Outback with Jesus, (Fort Worth: Harvest Press Inc., 1975).

Organic Gardening & Farming, Rodale Press Publications, Emmaus, Pennsylvania.

Natural Food and Farming Journal, Natural Food Associaties, Box 210, Atlanta, Texas.

New Earth - Journal of the Whole Life, Box 10225 Dallas, Texas 76207

New Harvest, poetry, prose and praise of the Spirit, Harvest Press, P.O.Box 3535, Fort Worth, Texas 76105

Rutstrum, Calvin, The Wilderness Cabin, (New York: Macmillian Publishing., Inc., 1901).

Some Natural Foods Sources

Akin Distributors, Inc.
  P. O. Box 2747, Tulsa, Okla. 74101
Arrowhead Mills Inc.
  Box 866, Hereford, Texas 79045
Arrowhead Mills Distributing Co.
  4255 Kearney St., Denver, Col. 80216
Ceres Natural Foods
  2582 Durango Drive, Colorado Springs, Col.80910
Cinagro Distributors
  3588 Pierce Dr., Chamblee, Ga. 30341
Collegedale Distributors
  P. O. Box 626, Collegedale, Tenn. 37315
Deer Valley Farms
  Rural Delivery One, Guilford, N. Y. 13780
Earth Bound, Inc.
  29 Pomperang Road, Woodbury, Ct. 06798
Earthwonder
  Star Rt. One, Box 92, Blue Eye, Mo. 65611
Eden Organic Foods
  4601 Platt Road, Ann Arbor, Mi. 48104
Erewhon Trading Company
  33 Farnsworth St., Boston, Mass. 02210
Erewhon Trading Company
  8454 Steller Drive, Culver, City, Cal. 90320
Food for Health
  P.O. Box 23122, Phoenix, Ariz. 85063
Food for Life
  420 Wrightwood Ave., Elmhurst, Ill. 60126
The Good Food People
  10001 Mc Kalla Place, Austin, Tex. 78758
Happy Health Products
  7875 N. W. 77th Ave., Medley, Fla. 33166
Health Foods, Inc.
  155 W. Higgins, Des Plaines, Ill. 60018
Houston Health Food Distributors
  4220 Pinemont, Houston, Texas 77018
Janus Natural Foods
  1523 Airport Way So., Seattle, Wash. 98134
Kahan & Lessin Co., 3131 E. Maria St.,
  Compton, Cal. 90221
Kozek Produce Co., 651 S. Kohler,
  Los Angeles, Cal. 90021

Landstrom Co., 336 Oyster Pt. Blvd. S.
   San Francisco, Cal. 94080
Laurelbrook Foods No. 1
   Box 47, Bel Air, Md. 21014
Laurelbrook Foods No. 2
   330 W. Davie St., Raleigh, N. C. 27603
Lifestream Natural Foods
   1241 Vulcan Way, Richmond, B.C., Canada
Manna Foods
   112 Crockford Blvd., Scarborough, Ont. Canada
   MIR 3C3
Midwest Natural Foods
   P. O. Box 100, Ann Arbor, Mi. 48107
Mottel Health Foods
   451 Washington St., New York, N.Y. 10013'
Naturally Good Foods
   Box 1892, Hereford, Texas 79045
Natures Best
   615 Nash St., El Segundo, Cal. 90245
Nu-Vita Foods, Inc.
   7524 S.W. Macadam Ave., Portland, Ore. 97219
Organic Foods & Gardens
   2655 Commerce Way,
   City of Commerce, Cal. 90040
Pure & Simple
   795 West Hedding, San Jose, Cal. 95126
Shadowfax
   25 N. Depot St., Binghamton, N.Y. 13901
Shiloh Farms, Inc.
   Box 97, Sulphur Springs, Ar. 72768
Shiloh Farms, Inc. Eastern Warehouse
   White Oak Rd., Martindale, Pa.
   (Near New Holland) 17549
The Wide Earth Store
   3903 Greenland Drive, Anchorage, Ala. 99503
Tochi Products
   1107 2nd Ave. N., Fargo, N. D. 58102
Taiyo, Inc.
   P.O. Box 3945, Honolulu, Hawaii 96812
Tree of Life
   315 Industrial Dr., St. Augustine, Fla. 32084
Walnut Acres, Inc.
   P. O. Box 8, Penns Creek, Pa. 17862

INDEX
OF RECIPES